THE MALTREATED CHILD

If a better world is to be tomorrow
— it will come through the hope
and future of today's children.

THE MALTREATED CHILD

The Maltreatment Syndrome in Children
A Medical, Legal and Social Guide

Fourth Edition

By

VINCENT J. FONTANA, M.D., F.A.A.P.

*Pediatrician in Chief and Medical Director
New York Foundling Hospital Center for
Parent and Child Development
Professor of Clinical Pediatrics
New York University
College of Medicine
New York, New York*

and

DOUGLAS J. BESHAROV, J.D., LL.M.

*Director
United States National Center of
Child Abuse and Neglect
Washington, D.C.*

With a Foreword by

Mother Loretto Bernard

*Mother General
Sisters of Charity of New York*

CHARLES C THOMAS • PUBLISHER

Springfield • Illinois • U.S.A.

Published and Distributed Throughout the World by
CHARLES C THOMAS • PUBLISHER
Bannerstone House
301-327 East Lawrence Avenue, Springfield, Illinois, U.S.A.

© *1964, 1971, 1977 and 1979 by* CHARLES C THOMAS • PUBLISHER
ISBN 0-398-03904-6
Library of Congress Catalog Card Number: 78-27727

First Edition, 1964
Second Edition, 1971
Second Edition, Second Printing, 1972
Second Edition, Third Printing, 1974
Third Edition, 1977
Fourth Edition, 1979

With THOMAS BOOKS *careful attention is given to all details of
manufacturing and design. It is the Publisher's desire to present books that
are satisfactory as to their physical qualities and artistic possibilities and
appropriate for their particular use.* THOMAS BOOKS *will be true to those
laws of quality that assure a good name and good will.*

Printed in the United States of America
V-R-1

Library of Congress Cataloging in Publication Data

Fontana, Vincent J
The maltreated child.

Includes indexes.
1. Child abuse. 2. Child abuse--Prevention.
I. Besharov, Douglas J., joint author.
II. Title. [DNLM: 1. Child abuse. 2. Child
welfare--United States. WA320 F679m]
HV713.F6 1979   362.7'1   78-27727
ISBN 0-398-03904-6

To

SISTER MARY IRENE FITZGIBBON

First Superior of the New York Foundling Hospital, whose faith, vision and indomitable courage laid the foundation of the great institution in which the Sisters of Charity of New York for over a century have lavished love and motherly care upon more than 115,000 abandoned, neglected or maltreated infants and children

FOREWORD

IT is a tragic commentary on the mental and moral health of our nation that the most common cause of childhood deaths today is physical abuse of children by their own parents. This shocking revelation, like the murder of our President and the racial bitterness that threatens civil war, should disturb our social conscience and prompt vigorous, intelligent action.

In *The Maltreated Child*, Dr. Vincent J. Fontana, Pediatrician in Chief and Medical Director of the New York Foundling Hospital Center for Parent and Child Development, analyzes the situation and outlines his work in abuse detection and therapy. Dr. Fontana has secured legislation in New York State that will rescue children from life-threatening home environments. As he phrases it: "We fail with leukemia; we fail with Hodgkins Disease; but this is one childhood disease that is in our power to conquer. And conquer it we will."

Every age has its men of vision and dedication. For more than a century, the selfless collaboration of men like Dr. Fontana has been the inspiration of the Sisters of Charity of New York in their difficult work of rehabilitating "battered children" in their hospitals and child-care homes. Never has this collaboration been more needed, more sustaining or more appreciated than it is today.

MOTHER LORETTO BERNARD
Mother General
Sisters of Charity of New York

vii

PREFACE TO FOURTH EDITION

THE recognition that child maltreatment is a major serious medical, social and legal problem in our nation and throughout the world has been realized and accepted by professionals in all disciplines dealing with child welfare. Within the past several years this recognition has resulted in positive and effective ways of combatting, preventing and treating child abuse through the establishment of innovative programs directed toward the rehabilitation of the abusive parents and the children. These programs include the use of a multidisciplinary approach utilizing intensive intervention and treatment.

Most recently the recognition that prenatal assessment of "high risk" parents and early intervention prevents future episodes of child maltreatment, has provided us with new tools to stem the increasing incidence of child abuse in this country.

The sexual abuse and exploitation of children which has been secretive, has begun to surface and is being recognized by authorities as an important medical-social family problem with psychosocial, legal, and medical implications. Through close cooperation with the judicial and protective systems, specific strategies of intervention have been developed for the management of sexual child abuse cases.

In view of these new advances in the field, it was felt important to re-edit the MALTREATED CHILD in order to provide current information to the professionals concerned and involved with the tragedy of child abuse.

In recognition of the International Year of the Child (1979) this new edition is dedicated to further heighten professional awareness to the plight of troubled families and children in crisis. The authors hope that an organized effort can be taken by all child caring individuals to ensure that:

"The child shall be protected against all forms of neglect,
cruelty, and exploitation" (Principle 9, the United Nations
Declaration of the Rights of the Child)

VINCENT J. FONTANA, M.D.

PREFACE TO THIRD EDITION

THIRTEEN years ago, when the first edition of this book appeared, there were only a handful of specialized resources in the entire country to help the maltreated child and his parents. The situation is quite different today. Many hundreds of books and articles have been written on the subject. All states have reporting laws regarding child abuse and neglect; almost every state has a central register to facilitate the management of child protective cases. Today large numbers of abusing and neglecting parents and their children are being helped through individual and group therapy, day care, medical services, social services, homemaker services, parent aides and residential treatment programs . . . to name a few.

Our previous work in the field and the publication of the "Maltreatment Syndrome in Children" in the *New England Journal of Medicine* in 1963 has identified and provided the professionals with an all-encompassing description of child abuse that now includes all forms of neglect and abuse both physical and psychological. Acceptance of the term "maltreatment" has increased our visibility of the problem and enabled us to develop a better understanding of the psychodynamics of child abuse that has resulted in more meaningful therapeutic modalities to prevent the maltreatment syndrome in children.

We have come a long way in the last thirteen years. And yet, we still have a long way to go before we can say we are providing adequate and effective services for the majority of maltreated children and their parents.

The purpose of this text remains the same as it was when it was first published. It seeks to present in a clear and concise way the problems of child maltreatment, their nature, causes, and extent and the means to deal with them. It is meant as a guide for those professionals and paraprofessionals responsible

xi

for the prevention and treatment of this serious medical-social syndrome. In this third edition, in recognition of the broadened role of law as a framework for the child protective process, additional materials on the legal process have been added. In addition, all the information in the book has been updated to reflect new developments in research and service programs.

I do not believe that the child abuse problem in this country with all its complexities and variations can be solved by any one single approach, since we are dealing not only with a complex problem but a multiplicity of human personalities and motivations. Just as there is no one cause of child abuse, there certainly cannot be one treatment. We will need every social, medical and governmental resource working collectively in the future to effectively control the child abuse problem in any community and for that matter, in this country. To achieve any amount of success, massive programs on parenting and family care, standardized in quality with emphasis on prevention and early detection, must be effectively developed by the medical, legal and social disciplines responsible for child welfare in this country.

VINCENT J. FONTANA, M.D., F.A.A.P.
DOUGLAS J. BESHAROV, J.D., LL.M.

PREFACE TO SECOND EDITION

SOCIAL awareness of child abuse in the last decade has resulted in the passage of child abuse laws in every state of this nation. However, in spite of these laws, the plight of the abused and neglected child has not been lessened and there has been an apparent increase in the number of child abuse cases reported throughout the country.

Much has been written on the subject since this text was first published in 1964. This second edition of *The Maltreated Child* has been expanded to include current concepts of child abuse, its diagnosis and management. The reference list in this edition has been updated to include all current information on the subject of child abuse and neglect.

The purpose of this text remains the same, namely to present in a concise and clear manner the problem of child abuse and to familiarize students, medical house officers, physicians, social workers, teachers, nurses and lawyers with this all important medical-social syndrome.

VINCENT J. FONTANA

PREFACE TO FIRST EDITION

In 1869, the first institution was established in a large city to arrest the crime of child murder. The name chosen gave adequate testimony of its purpose — The Home for Foundlings, and it was started by Sister Mary Irene and her two companions, Sister Theresa Vincent and Sister Ann Aloysia.

This refuge for abandoned infants brought society closer to the apparent high incidence of the heartless, deliberate sacrifice of unwanted children by their parents. These children of vice, immorality and poverty were then, and are now, at the mercy of parental inadequacies.

My appointment to the position of Medical Director and Pediatrician in Chief at the New York Foundling Hospital brought me closer to the plight of the neglected and unwanted child. Through the energies of the Sisters of Charity, thousands of children have been saved from imminent mental and physical damage and placed into the protective, secure and happy surroundings of the Foundling Hospital.

In these times of apparent material abundance, it is hard to believe that children are being neglected and maltreated by their parents.

Dr. Kempe's article in 1962, in the *Journal of the American Medical Association*, further enlightened the public and the medical profession to the startling high incidence of the battered child in our society. A greater number of mistreated children than reported are probably going unrecognized, undetected and unprotected.

This pediatric disease is probably causing the greatest number of deaths in children. Very little can be done for the child suffering with cancer, except to perhaps prolong his life for a while; however, the child being abused and neglected can be saved from possible death by adequate recognition and protection. This thought prompted my interest in the field of parental delinquency and the maltreatment of children. Prior to my exposure to the abandoned, unwanted, neglected and abused child, I too, could not accept that such unbelievable inhuman behavior existed in our present-day modern society. Further study and personal experiences with the problem of the maltreated child revealed a series of incidents filled with corrupt, sadistic, psychosocial aberrations leading to the willful abuse of children.

Behind closed doors a countless number of helpless young children and infants are being abused, neglected and often battered by parents or other individuals in the family. These children are beaten with instruments ranging from bare fists to baseball bats; others are being burned over open flames, gas burners and cigarette lighters; some are strangled; others are suffocated with pillows or plastic bags, and some are being drowned.

In discussing this problem with other physicians, it became apparent that a blind spot existed concerning the importance of frequency of this pediatric entity. I also realize that society, social workers, public health officials and law enforcement agencies have failed to recognize the maltreatment syndrome in children, partly because of their disbelief. They also are unable to accept the fact that such brutality exists, partly because of inadequate knowledge and training in the recognition of the child afflicted with this syndrome.

In my experience with the family courts, I was continuously confronted with the concept that "a child's place is with its mother." This type of thinking has led to many children being returned to helpless, sick parents and life-threatening environments.

It is therefore the purpose of this book to bring out from hiding the types of abuse and neglect inflicted on children and the diagnostic criteria which can confirm the physician's suspicions. The medical, social and legal responsibilities are also discussed. There is an urgent need for society to recognize parental delinquency, to face up to the fact that inhuman treatment of children by their parents does exist in a civilized society.

There must be a recognition of and concern for this problem among medical, legal and social leaders. There must be a drive by all phases of society to decrease and eventually eradicate this outrageous crime of child abuse. This disease could become a rarity if all suspected cases were reported by physicians, social workers, hospital administrators and members of our community.

The maltreatment syndrome in children is one of the leading causes of death in pediatrics. This useless and needless death of children can and should be prevented. The countless number of children being crippled and killed by inflicted trauma must be salvaged if our society is to survive. The future hope and strength of our children lies in the cooperative efforts of the medical, social and legal systems of our country.

This is a most disturbing problem confronting our society today; its solution lies in the eradication of ignorance — an overwhelming national grievance of child abuse. Our society at present does not want to face the hard facts of child abuse; the associated apathy and ignorance on the subject has resulted in the continued insidious surge of battered children.

This book has been written with the hope and conviction that something must be and can be done to prevent child abuse and death. It is up to every member of society to see that this disease is removed from our midst.

VINCENT J. FONTANA

ACKNOWLEDGMENTS

I WISH to express my gratitude to Sister Cecilia Schneider, Executive Director of the New York Foundling Hospital Center for Parent and Child Development, for her foresight and leadership in the development of the first Temporary Shelter for Abusing Parents in the United States. My sincere appreciation to my loyal secretary Miss Anne Dougherty for the many years of patient and dedicated efforts in the preparation and coordination of the manuscript.

V.J.F.

CONTENTS

THE MALTREATED CHILD

"Mankind owes to the child — the best it has to give."

— *United Nations Charter*

"Kill not your children for fear of being brought to want."

— *Mohammed*

"Suffer the little children to come unto me and forbid them not; for of such is the kingdom of God."

— *Luke 18:16*

"In the little world in which children have their existence, whosoever brings them up, there is nothing so finely perceived and so finely felt as injustice."

— *Charles Dickens*

"We have been told that in America's children lies the strength, the hope and the future of our country. We mean all of America's children especially those forsaken babies who are innocent victims of human weakness and misfortune."

— *Francis Cardinal Spellman*

1

HISTORICAL DATA

THE neglect and abuse of children has been evidenced since the beginning of time. The natural animalistic instincts of the human race have not changed with the passing of the centuries. Children have been crippled and killed either through ignorance or superstition, by shame or in secrecy. This wastage of children's lives continues and appears to be increasing even in this enlightened modern day.

Infanticide, the killing of newborn infants by suffocation, drowning or exposure to the elements, was accepted by previous societies, particularly in the seventeenth century. Unwanted children were easily disposed of without any incrimination or guilt. In some societies it was a regular practice to destroy all physically handicapped babies. Infanticide may also have been practiced as a form of birth control. In Greece and Rome the practice was also apparent; the abandoned infant was often left exposed in an open place. These infants were left in conspicuous locations and mythology relates tales of heroes who began life as infants exposed to die. With the advances in medicine, science and social conditions, the special needs of children during the nineteenth and early twentieth centuries have been recognized. Society has recognized the need to supply children with the care, protection and education they deserve, but these needs are still unfulfilled.

For many years, the responsibility for the protection of children has been generally ignored, and no adequate measures have been taken to treat those involved in these intolerable acts of childhood abuse and neglect.

In 1869, the Roman Catholic Order of the Sisters of Charity of St. Vincent De Paul founded the New York Foundling Hospital, the first institution to be established in a large city in the United States providing a refuge for abandoned, neglected and abused children.

3

The prime objective of the Foundling Hospital was realized, in that the appalling rate of infanticide in New York City was drastically reduced after its doors were opened.

In the first year of operation, the New York Foundling Hospital received 1,060 infants, 61 percent admitted were *in extremis*.

Through the years, over 200,000 helpless, abused, neglected and abandoned children have found refuge and love within this institution. Today, the Foundling Hospital's Center for Parent and Child Development is still in the forefront of society's efforts to protect children and help parents. It is the home of one of the first comprehensive residential programs for parent and child to treat and prevent child abuse by helping parents while protecting their children.

As a result of the writings of Kempe, who coined the term "battered child syndrome" in 1962, and the author's description of the "maltreatment syndrome" in 1963, the problems of child abuse have been given the highest priority by medical, legal and social professional groups as a major, unsolved health problem in our children. The battered child syndrome has been recognized as the most severe form of child abuse which lies at the end of the spectrum of child maltreatment due to insufficient parental care and protection.

The true seriousness of the problem in our society is appreciated by the involvement of the American Academy of Pediatrics, the Children's Bureau, the American Humane Society and other medical and social groups throughout the nation. The judicial and legal authorities have also recognized the importance of protecting the rights of a child. The true incidence of this maltreatment of children is more accurate today in view of child abuse laws that mandate reporting in all of the American states, the District of Columbia and the Virgin Islands. This disease of our times has shown a steady increase in recent years. The news media, radio, television and the press have presented the problem of the battered child and the resulting fatalities. These presentations have stimulated a concerted effort by society to become involved and to help eradicate the willfully inflicted trauma and damage upon helpless children by their parents or other persons responsible for their care.

In 1972, the Committee on Infant and Preschool Child of the American Academy of Pediatrics issued a statement indicating that "while a great deal of study and activity has taken place with regard to the problem of the battered child and there have been some positive results, the consensus of the Committee and its consultants is that the total problem has become magnified and is uncontrolled by present methods of management."

In 1974, President Richard Nixon signed into law federal legislation, PL 93-247, the Child Abuse Prevention and Treatment Act, which established the United States National Center on Child Abuse and Neglect in Washington, D.C.

During the 1970s, a variety of demonstration treatment and prevention programs were developed throughout the country as a result of our more complete knowledge of the psychodynamics of child abuse and the monies made available through the implementation of the PL 93-247, the Child Abuse Prevention and Treatment Act of 1974. The variety of innovative approaches to the treatment and prevention of child abuse include community child protective services, crisis- or hotlines for parents in times of crisis, a crisis nursery to provide children with a refuge for protection, hospital child abuse teams, lay therapy or parent-aide programs, day care and preschool programs for children, self-help groups such as Parents Anonymous, and residential treatment crisis intervention centers for the whole family.

2

THE "MALTREATMENT SYNDROME" IN CHILDREN

THE maltreatment of children is vigorously increasing and has become one of the world's most desperate problems. The maltreatment syndrome in children must be recognized by our society regardless of social or economic background, ages or outward appearances of a child's parents. Today, under child abuse laws in the United States, whenever a case of abuse and neglect is suspected, it must be reported and investigated with all possible speed. Abuse and neglect of children are medical-social problems of major proportion that are plaguing society by killing and crippling untold numbers of defenseless children.

This maltreatment has been hidden medically and socially for many years, and in view of the obvious ignorance about the subject, it has also been hidden statistically until recently. The maltreatment of children had not been considered important enough to be included in the curricula of medical schools; it had not been given notice in any of the major pediatric textbooks; and it had been ignored by both society and physicians for many years. This seems to be a result of society's disbelief that such inhuman cruelties could willfully be inflicted upon children. The physician has been deficient in his recognition and diagnosis of these cases due to lack of information and/or a desire to protect his patient from embarrassment based on little evidence or mere suspicion. There are also physicians who have not reported such cases, since they have feared involvement in court action or legal entanglements which could even lead to suits of malpractice. In the last decade, however, medical schools, pediatric texts and physicians have shown more awareness of the problem of child abuse, because of recent publications on the subject by Kempe, Fontana, Silverman, Steele, DeFrancis, Helfer and others.

6

The maltreatment of children encompasses all forms of inflicted "hurt" to a child, both physical and/or psychological, caused by parental abuse or neglect. The types of neglect may be physical, medical and/or emotional. Inflicted abuse includes the physical, emotional and sexual maltreatment of a child.

The relationship of sexual abuse to the maltreatment of children has not been emphasized or carefully documented. However, the New York State Child Protective Service Act enacted into law in 1973 clearly included in the definition of the "abused child" anyone under the age of sixteen years "whose parent or other person legally responsible for his care commits or allows to be committed against the child an act of sexual abuse as defined in the penal law." Although the law may show concern for children who are sexually assaulted, the child protective agencies are oftentimes not able to intervene voluntarily without consent of the parent, except in situations in which there is suspicious parental culpability. Ms. Carol J. Parry, Assistant Commissioner of Special Services for Children in New York City, reported that of a total of 26,500 children reported to the Special Registry in 1975 for suspected maltreatment, more than 540 were subsequently identified as victims of alleged sexual abuse.

In a report by Vincent De Francis in 1969, 1,000 children that were victims of child abuse were studied and it was found that a member of the household was the sexual offender in 27 percent of the instances, and 37 percent were friends or acquaintances of the family. Another important relationship was noted in this study; namely, that in 11 percent of these families physical abuse was also directed toward the child, and child neglect was noted in 79 percent of the families. The sexual abuse of a child should be considered within the context of maltreatment as another form of violent parental behavior directed toward the older child when adolescent sexuality may trigger such a parental response. Recent statistics do indicate however that the problem of sexual abuse can affect children on all age levels ranging from two months to seventeen years of age. The average age of the reported victimized child in New York City was ten and one-half years. Exact statistics are not available in view of the "hidden" character of the abuse, the invisibility of the perpetrators, and the fear, shame and guilt of the victim and of the family members. State laws require reporting of suspected cases of child maltreatment generally and sexual abuse specifically.

The statistical problem is compounded further by some physicians who not only resist recognizing sexual abuse when it confronts them, but also by their refusing to report it; families' fear of dissolution if the abuse is revealed; and by courts insisting upon rules of evidence so strict as to result in low conviction rates.

In sexual abuse, as in physical child abuse, incestuous families are usually multitroubled. The parents are no longer the child's protectors but the child's offenders. All maltreated children, whether abused physically, sexually or emotionally, suffer at the hands of their family because most children have no "bail out" capabilities and no power or access to community resources that might help them. According to some sociologists, such abusive treatment of children is inherent in the basic inequality of physical make-up and social status that exist between adults and children.

Within a family practicing incest, the mother figure is usually the controlling force. Whenever she fails to protect the child by playing a passive approving role, she either consciously or unconsciously sanctions the incestuous activity. Thus, in allowing the abuse to continue, she plays a critical role in the context of the disturbed family system. Within the family, there may also be a series of child maltreatment incidents, a broad pattern of interfamilial crisis, disorganization, maladjustment, sexual difficulties between parents and a lack of acceptance of the established social values of the particular community.

Cases of sexual abuse are especially difficult to diagnose because the participants are sworn to secrecy and the continuing sexual relationship is controlled by one who is usually in authority over the victim. The involved parents may have experienced emotional or physical deprivation during their own childhood. For these parents, the threat of a family breakup only intensifies their stress and inhibitions, making it even less likely that the case will be reported. Carrying this sex-stressful burden will cause the victim to gradually withdraw from social and interfamilial activities. It can also build up interpersonal tensions to the point that they ultimately reveal their "shameful secret" to the authorities.

Society's present level of understanding and refusal to accept the sexual abuse problem can be compared to its reluctance to accept the battered child problem in the 1960s. The syndrome of sexual abuse, including incest and molestation, usually leaves no physical scars. X-rays do not show any bone damage diagnostic of physical abuse. Today an unwilling, defensive society would prefer dealing with sexual abuse by denying its existence or by prosecuting the abuser. The attitude guarantees not only the continued sexual abuse of children, but also that it will go undetected and unreported.

One can readily see then that the most important aspect of this disease is that many of the maltreated children who survive will have future emotional and psychological crippling which is passed on to succeeding generations — along with a sense of rejection and frustration leading to further crimes and violence in our society and to a future generation of violent, angry parents. It has also been theorized that children so maltreated have an unusual degree of hostility towards parents and toward the world in general. It would appear, therefore — although certainly more investigative work is necessary and wanting to come to any reliable conclusions — that the maltreatment of children may well provide one of the sources of juvenile delinquency, future murderers and perpetrators of violence in our society. Strong consideration should be given to the thesis that treating the syndrome of the maltreated child may be a means of preventing not only possible permanent physical or mental injury or death of a child but may also be a means of breaking the violence breeding violence generational cycle.

3

STATISTICS

AN editorial in the *Journal of the American Medical Association* stated that the maltreatment of children, if statistics were complete and available, could possibly turn out to be

a more frequent cause of death than such well recognized and thoroughly studied diseases as leukemia, cystic fibrosis and muscular dystrophy, and may even rank with automobile accidents and the toxic and infectious encephalitis, as causes of atypical disturbances of the central nervous system.

The U.S. National Vital Statistics Division listed cancer as the major cause of pediatric deaths in 1959. Accidental deaths among children during the same year actually ranked 175 percent higher. The question arises as to how many of these so-called accidental deaths were due to the unsuspected maltreatment of children.

Dr. Henry C. Kempe of the University of Colorado School of Medicine (1962) reported the results of a nationwide survey of hospitals and law enforcement agencies which indicated the high incidence of battered children within a one-year period. A total of 749 children were reported maltreated. Of this number, 78 children died and 114 suffered permanent brain damage. In only one third of these cases, proper medical diagnosis initiated court action. Kempe also indicated that the maltreatment of children was a particularly common problem in his hospital and on a single day the pediatric service of the Colorado General Hospital was caring for four infants suffering from parent-inflicted injuries.

A study of the Massachusetts Society for the Prevention of Cruelty to Children showed that in 1960 over two hundred children had been referred to the agency for investigation of child abuse. Only 9 percent of the cases had been referred by hospitals and doctors though more than 30 percent of the

10

abused children had received medical care.

In New York City, where approximately two thousand children await placement, in 1962 over five thousand dependency and neglect cases came to the attention of the children's court.

The Children's Division of the American Humane Society studied the number of child abuse cases reported in the newspapers of the country in 1962, and reported a total of 662 children who had been maltreated. Approximately one in every four children, or a total of 148 children, died as a result of the inflicted injuries. Perhaps for every case of maltreatment that makes the newspapers, there are from 50 to 100 abused or neglected children that go without attention.

Another survey conducted by the Children's Bureau showed 447 cases in the first half of 1961 resulting in 45 deaths and 29 brain injuries. The Cook County Family Court, which covers Chicago and its suburbs, reported receiving about one hundred cases each month. The admission rate of physically abused children at Cook County Hospital was approximately ten a day. Offices of the chief medical examiners have also been aware of a rise in childhood deaths probably resulting from maltreatment.

The Reverend William Kalaidjian, President of the Bronx County Society for the Prevention of Cruelty to Children in New York, stated in his annual report that "in 1969, private agency figures of the Societies for the Prevention of Cruelty to Children in New York City indicated that approximately 15,772 children that had been abused, neglected or harmed in varying degrees were reported to the Society's Brooklyn, Manhattan and Bronx County offices."

Walter F. Mondale from Minnesota, Former Chairman of the Subcommittee on Children and Youth, has stated that each year some 60,000 children in this country are reported to have been abused. Dr. Vincent De Francis, Director of the Children's Division of the American Humane Association, estimates that there are between 30,000 and 40,000 cases of truly "battered children" reported annually and suggests that there are at least 100,000 who are sexually abused and 200,000 to 300,000 children who

are psychologically abused each year. Dr. Ray Helfer has estimated, based on a 20 percent increase of child abuse reported
cases, that the next decade will bring forth 1.5 million cases of
suspected maltreatment reports, 50,000 childhood deaths and a
minimum of 300,000 permanently injured children.

A continued annual increase in child abuse reports have been
noted in the New York City Central Registry's statistical report
of abuse and neglect allegations. From January 1975 to December 1975, there was a dramatic increase in the reported cases
especially in the abuse category — a total of 26,536 cases of
child maltreatment reported as compared with a total of 22,683
in 1974. This social-medical problem has assumed critical epi-
demic proportion in New York, a city with a large alcohol- and
drug-addicted population, high unemployment rate and the
stressful living conditions of the ghettos. A conservative esti-
mate is that at least 150 children in New York City die each
year as a result of maltreatment. In 1974, the New York Central
Registry reported 115 deaths attributable to suspected parental
maltreatment. In the United States, two thousand or more
children die every year as a result of parental abuse and neglect.

Information available today strongly indicates that as many
as one million children are being maltreated in a variety of
ways, ranging from gross neglect and starvation to physical and
mental cruelty leading to the physical and emotional damage
of the child. Child abuse and neglect has become a widespread,
violent, childrearing pattern which is becoming more en-
trenched in our population.

Child abuse is a symptom of the violence running rampant
in American society today. If it is allowed to continue at its
present pace, it will threaten the future of our families and the
entire fabric of our civilization. Child abuse is one form of
violence which results in social disorganization and disintegra-
tion. Persons who engage in violence tend to have been victims
of violence. This generation's battered children, if they survive,
may well become the next generation's battering parents. It has
been shown that many infants and young children that have
been abused and neglected at the hands of their own parents —
if they survive — tend to carry out their injuries into adoles-

cence. As these children begin to approach adolescence they show evidence of the psychological and emotional disturbances leading to juvenile delinquency. Dr. Karl Menninger has stated that "every criminal was an unloved and maltreated child." He feels that the criminal is the child who survives his maltreatment physically but who suffers at the hands of unrestrained, aggressive and psychotic adults.

It appears that the story of the proverbial submerged iceberg is a dramatic example of the true incidence of the maltreatment syndrome in children. This lack of true statistics is due to a variety of factors: Parents make up believable stories; children are usually too young or too frightened to disclose what actually happened; and some physicians are shocked by the idea that parents would abuse and destroy their children and would rather attribute symptoms to an accident or a disease than to actual inflicted abuse. Other doctors tend to shut their eyes because they fear legal complications. The children's court judges, many of whom are not fully informed on this problem, usually return the young victim to his parents with a light reprimand and a look of disbelief for the physician who testified in the case. In recent years both the reluctant physician and the disbelieving judge have become more aware of the actuality of child abuse.

Accurate statistics concerning the incidence of this pediatric entity are unobtainable since only a portion of neglected and abused children are taken to the hospitals for medical attention.

This pediatric disease is preventable. A sustained and determined effort should be made in all parts of the country, through the mass media of medical education and through the formal education channels, to awaken the general public to the problem of maltreatment of children. Efforts must be made to persuade those who are involved in this type of abuse to report and seek social, medical and legal assistance. The maltreatment syndrome of children is an intolerable disease and can be eradicated through definite measures and through cooperative integrated efforts by the medical, social and legal disciplines of our society.

The first case of child abuse recorded in New York was that

of a child named Mary Ellen, whose inhuman treatment caused the early public outpouring of shock and sympathy for the maltreated child. A church worker, while visiting an aged woman in a tenement house, learned that this little girl was beaten daily. She was told that the child appeared to be seriously malnourished and showed evidence of neglect and abuse. The church worker's efforts to help Mary Ellen and remove her from her environment, after making contact with the protective agencies including the police and the district attorney's office, proved useless. In desperation, this woman appealed to Henry Bergh, a member of the American Society for the Prevention of Cruelty to Animals. She pointed out that this child, for all practical purposes, was being treated as an animal and was certainly a member of the animal kingdom. The Society for the Prevention of Cruelty to Animals brought action resulting in this child's subsequent removal from the parents, who were afflicting the abuse and maltreatment.

In 1875, one year later, the New York Society for the Prevention of Cruelty to Children was organized. It is a sad commentary that it took a society for the prevention of cruelty to animals to protect the first maltreated child on record.

Reported cases of the maltreatment syndrome in children have been increasing at the rate of 15 to 20 percent throughout the United States. This trend is not confined to any race, sex, socioeconomic group or geographic area. This problem exists throughout the world. It is, therefore, the purpose of the monograph to state our present understanding of the maltreatment syndrome in children, the medical criteria necessary for diagnosis, the social implications to this disease and the medical, social and legal responsibilities that must be fulfilled in order to prevent these unnecessary deaths of children.

4

DIAGNOSIS

WITHIN the last several years, there has been a medical awareness of a critical pediatric problem involving the neglect and abuse of children. The infliction of serious injuries to children is not a new entity in medicine, but has existed since the beginning of time. Only recently there has been an apparent increased incidence of maltreated children reported in the medical literature and noted by child protective agencies throughout the country. Prior to these reports, this pediatric syndrome of the maltreated child has for the most part gone unrecognized by the authorities. Little or no information on the subject was available in the standard pediatric and medical texts.

The neglect and abuse of children denotes a situation ranging from the deprivation of food, clothing, shelter and parental love to incidences where children are physically abused and mistreated by an adult, resulting in obvious physical trauma to the child and not infrequently leading to death.

Many of these children who are seen by the physicians go unreported, or are recorded as cases of accidental trauma. Kempe has described this repeated physical abuse of children as the battered child syndrome. Other reports in medical literature have referred to this disease of maltreatment as "unrecognized trauma," "traumatic periostitis," "traumatization of children," "parent induced trauma" and "unsuspected trauma." Unfortunately none of these terms fully describes the true picture of this often life-threatening condition. A more precise and descriptive term that should be applied to this clinical entity is "the maltreatment syndrome in children." A maltreated child often presents itself without obvious signs of being battered but with the multiple minor physical evidences of emotional and, at times, nutritional deprivation, neglect and abuse. The battered child is only the last phase of the spectrum of the maltreatment syn-

15

drome.

In cases of maltreatment of children, the most acute diagnostic acumen of the physician can prevent the more serious and severe injuries due to inflicted trauma that are a significant cause of childhood deaths. It must be emphasized that the willful neglect and injury of these children by parents or caretakers may range from the child who is malnourished or physically neglected to the victim of premeditated trauma leading to crippling or death. Awareness by physicians, nurses, social workers, teachers, clergy and hospital administrators of the signs and symptoms of the maltreatment syndrome, a preventable disease, can be life saving.

CLINICAL MANIFESTATIONS

The maltreated child is often brought to the hospital or private physician with a history of failure to thrive: malnutrition, anemia, poor skin hygiene, irritability, a repressed personality and other signs of obvious neglect. The more severely abused children are seen in the emergency rooms of hospitals with external evidences of body trauma: bruises, abrasions, cuts, lacerations, burns, soft tissue swelling and hematomas. Inability to move certain extremities because of dislocations and fractures associated with neurological signs of intercranial damage are additional signals that should arouse the suspicion of the attending physician. Children manifesting the maltreatment syndrome give evidence of one or more of these complaints with the most severe of the maltreatment cases arriving at the hospital or at the physician's office in coma, convulsions or even dead.

Therefore, the signs and symptoms apparent in the maltreatment of children range from the simple undernourished infant who is reported as "failing to thrive" to the more severely battered child who is seen with evidence of multiple fractures and inflicted trauma. Soft tissue lacerations, abrasions, burns and hematomas involving any part of the body should cast suspicion on the etiology of the presenting complaints. Even more enlightening is the presence of healed or scab-covered old abrasions or contusions of the skin. Manifestations of multiple vitamin deficiencies may also be evident in these children. Subdural hematomas associated with multiple skeletal fractures have been noted in some of these maltreated subjects. Caffey, in 1946, first reported the frequency of subdural hematoma in infants accompanied by fractures of the long bones. He described six patients with subdural hematoma who exhibited a total of twenty-three fractures and four contusions of the long bones. In not a single case was there a history of injury to which the skeletal lesions could reasonably be attributed, and in no case was there clinical or x-ray evidence of generalized or localized skeletal disease which would predispose to pathological fractures. Caffey later offered the possible explanation of parental neglect and abuse as a cause of this association of symptoms. Bakwin, Lis and Frauenberger in this country, Smith in Canada, and Marquezy and Marie in France have also noted this relationship between subdural hematoma and fracture of the long bones.

Kempe has stated that subdural hematoma, with or without fracture of the skull, is a frequent finding in these cases even in the absence of fracture of the long bones. The physician should therefore be alerted to the fact that the frequent occurrences of a typical fracture of the shaft or a long bone or rib, in the presence of an unusual metaphyseal lesion, should point to the diagnosis of inflicted trauma.

Any infant presenting with a subdural hematoma without a clear history of trauma should always receive a thorough skeletal survey to detect clinically silent dislocations, fractures and subperiosteal hemorrhages.

Other clinical signs and symptoms attributed to inflicted abuse may include injury to soft tissues and viscera. Inflicted abdominal trauma may result in "unexplained" rupture of stomach, bowel or liver with manifestations of an acute abdomen. Child abuse may also be noted in association with the maternal deprivation syndrome wherein x-ray signs of retarded development and clinical signs of neglect may coexist.

Maternal deprivation syndrome, a form of child maltreatment, can have serious and lifelong effects on the child's future growth and development if not diagnosed in the early stages. The only way to establish a cause and effect relationship between the infant's mothering and his symptoms is to demonstrate significant recovery when the mothering behavior is altered by immediate intervention or persistent surveillance of the child during a period of hospitalization. This single criteria confirms the diagnosis. All infants diagnosed as markedly deprived should have an investigation of the social-environmental condition of the family and the psychological status of the mother to determine the factors responsible for the child's deprivation and neglect.

Ocular damage is a common finding in the battered child and the diagnosis must be considered in all cases of severe retinal hemorrhage and optic atrophy in infants and young children. Periorbital swelling and ecchymosis, subconjunctival hemorrhages and disconjugate eye movements may also be evidence of direct ocular trauma.

Neurologic findings mimicking organic brain damage including exaggerated startle, hyperreflexia and increased muscle tone may be present in the battered child with no external signs of trauma.

The Office of Chief Medical Examiner, City of New York, has reported that the largest percentage of human bite marks encountered in the course of their forensic investigations has been found on battered-child homicide victims, most of whom exhibited multiple bite marks.

The nonaccidental poisoning of children must be considered in any child with unexplained symptoms. Symptoms of irritation of the central nervous system, convulsions and gastrointestinal symptomatology may confuse the unsuspecting physician. The correct diagnosis may be missed because incriminating evidence is not detected or recognized.

If the patient is hospitalized, blood, urine, stool and stomach washings should be made available for clinical testings. Sudden deaths associated with unexplained signs and symptoms necessitate a complete toxicology analysis.

Information about the child's presenting symptoms, history of drug addiction in household or drugs used by the parents, may help in making the diagnosis of child abuse. Parents who poison their children may have marital and/or psychiatric problems or may be abusing drugs themselves.

ROENTGENOLOGIC MANIFESTATIONS

Many of these children are not taken to the physician or hospital for medical care, because parents fear legal action, until the child is in acute distress or the parents become alarmed of impending death. For this reason, x-ray evidence of inflicted trauma may be present in various stages of reparative changes. The initial physical examination may be unrevealing, since the results of the bone injury may remain obscure during the first few days after the inflicted trauma. In these cases, evidences of bone repair make their appearance within weeks after specific bone trauma, and unless follow-up x-rays are taken, these diagnostic x-ray findings will go unnoticed. Unfortunately, because of the minimal signs accompanying most metaphyseal injuries, rarely will a physician's attention be called to the advisability of obtaining an x-ray. It is important to note that when an x-ray is obtained shortly after the traumatic episode, it may well be normal except for the presence of some soft tissue edema. Later, when the periosteal reactions contain calcium, the absence of clinical findings eliminates the need for further x-ray examination. In many of these cases of maltreatment, complete clinical recoveries take place. The initial incidence is therefore forgotten and the infant is returned to the parent.

General practitioners treat approximately 60 percent of the simple fractures incurred by children. They are therefore put in the responsible position of quickly identifying the presenting signs of unexplained multiple associated injuries. When a physician sees a child who has multiple injuries over many areas of the body and the history is not consistent with the physical findings observed, he must consider the possibility of maltreatment and should make the parents suspect.

The more common findings on x-ray examination of the long bones of these trauma cases reveal several diagnostic and unusual bone changes that have been described by Silverman and others. Metaphyseal fragmentation is caused by twisting or pulling of the afflicted extremity. There may be squaring of the long bones secondary to new bone formation on the metaphyseal fragments. Periosteal hemorrhages are frequently noted since the periosteum of infants is not securely attached to the underlying bone and is therefore easily lifted by the resulting hemorrhage after trauma. This is followed by periosteal calcification which begins to become apparent from five to seven days after the inflicted trauma. This layer of calcification, and later ossification, around the shaft of the bone should be evidence for suspicion of inflicted trauma, and further investigations to search for the etiological causes should be undertaken. The epiphyseal separations and periosteal shearing usually result from traction and torsion of the affected limb. The finding on x-ray or reparative changes involving excessive new bone formation or the presence of previously healed fractures with periosteal reactions may be diagnostic when correlated with the other manifestations of child abuse.

The presence of bone changes in several locations and in different stages of healing should be indicative of repeated episodes of trauma. When correlated with the history and social findings, it is usually confirmatory evidence in the diagnosis of the maltreatment syndrome.

Healing occurs rapidly after the source of inflicted trauma is eliminated. It is usually complete within four to twelve weeks, depending on the severity and duration of the injury. Children who have been followed with skeletal changes due to inflicted trauma have been noted to have no residual deformity after several months.

Caffey was the first to point out the frequency with which defects in the metaphysis contrasted to the shafts of the bone were encountered in the skeletal lesions in infants of traumatic origin. Astley, in England, described six babies with metaphyseal discontinuity of bone and the coincidental presence of retinal separation, easy bruising, black eyes, compressed vertebrae and the more unusual type of fractures.

Jones discussed and summarized forty-two cases of multiple

traumatic lesions of the infant skeleton and discussed accurately the various types of traumatic lesions in childhood. Most of his patients had ordinary fractures of either the shaft of the long bone or rib. It was the presence of the metaphyseal lesions, the appearance of which was striking, which aroused suspicion that something unusual was going on in these cases.

Many pediatricians, orthopedists and surgeons are not convinced that trauma may be responsible for the unusual bone changes that are seen on x-ray. For this reason, it is most important that the physician obtain a complete and reliable history, and seek social service investigative assistance in order to search into the etiology of any unexplained injuries to bones in children.

The physician must be aware that certain skeletal lesions are due to certain vectors of inflicted force which must be identified. Only through cooperative diagnostic efforts on the part of all physicians and social workers can the true incidence of this maltreatment syndrome in children be ascertained and efforts be made toward its prevention.

5

DIFFERENTIAL DIAGNOSIS

THE diagnosis of maltreatment of children is not an easy one to make, and may cause unnecessary grief to parents if made quickly and prematurely, or based solely on suspicion. The diagnosis must be made by history and a complete physical examination — only after thorough consultation with other physicians and discussion with the social service worker investigating the case.

In the differential diagnosis, the physician must rule out organic or accidental causes of the skeletal manifestations. These may be attributed to fractures and injuries associated with a prolonged and difficult labor in infancy. Unless the causes of the fractures or dislocations are obviously due to inflicted trauma, diseases such as scurvy, syphilis, infantile cortical hyperostosis, osteogenesis imperfecta and infectious osteitis as well as accidental trauma must be considered and ruled out.

Skeletal injuries on x-ray examination, whether accidental or inflicted, are most frequently confused with scurvy because of the presence of ossified subperiosteal hemorrhages. In scurvy, however, there are characteristic changes which usually are diagnostic. A ground glass osteoporosis, cortical thinning, and epiphyseal ringing are prominent findings in scurvy. It is also important to remember that scurvy almost never occurs during the first five months of life when traumatic injuries are most commonly noted.

In infantile cortical hyperostosis one usually notes tender swellings deep in the soft tissues associated with cortical thickening in the skeleton. This disease is usually seen during the first three months of life. On x-ray, hyperostosis usually involves the mandible, clavicles, scapulae, ribs and tubular bones of the extremities.

Infections, including tuberculosis and syphilis, can be ruled out by a history of infection, laboratory data indicating infection, bacteriological studies and skin tests. During the early months of life, the bone lesions of congenital syphilis may resemble those due to battering. However, the lesions due to syphilis are usually symmetrical, and are associated with the luetic stigmata, and the disease can be confirmed by serological testing.

In osteogenesis imperfecta, the manifestations are usually generalized with evidence of the disorder present in bones throughout the body. The fractures in osteogenesis imperfecta are commonly of the shafts. The presence of multiple fractures associated with blue sclera, skeletal deformities and of a family history of similar abnormalities usually confirms the diagnosis.

Neurologic signs, including exaggerated startle, and stretch reflex changes with retardation of development and growth, may mimic those of organic brain disease. The differential diagnosis, however, is easily made upon admission to a hospital. Functional neurological signs and symptoms rapidly disappear while the findings of organic nervous system do not.

Accidental trauma is common in children and should always be considered before making a diagnosis of inflicted injury. This consideration will oftentimes prevent faulty and unwarranted accusations of parents who bring their child to the attention of a physician.

The physician in charge of the case and the hospital child abuse committee must be sensitive to the seriousness of the diagnosis and the acute needs of these cases. They should recognize that a complete and thorough diagnostic evaluation is as important for these children as it is in the cause of fever of undetermined origin, diabetes, cancer and other illnesses.

Physicians need not be experts in the management of child maltreatment, but they should not overlook or miss a case of child abuse any more than they should miss an occasional case of Wilm's tumor or lymphoma. In both situations, prompt recognition and diagnosis may be life saving.

6

SOCIAL MANIFESTATIONS

THE maltreatment of children by parental abuse or neglect may occur at any age with an increased incidence in children under three years of age. In view of this, the abused infant or child cannot tell the story of how the trauma was inflicted and many young children are reluctant or afraid to tell the story.

The history that is related by the parents is very often at variance with the clinical picture and the physical findings noted on examination of the child. At times, parents are afraid to tell one another about the injury; a sitter, relative or nurse may be reluctant to report to the parent that an accident occurred; or the baby may be injured by older siblings. Injury, often deliberately inflicted by a parent or guardian, is difficult to elicit on history.

Information can only be brought out by prolonged and adroit questioning by the physician, social worker or hospital authority. Sometimes feelings of guilt cause the parents to withhold the true history. At times, the source of the inflicted trauma or neglect may be unknown to those customarily concerned with the care of the infant. Seeking out information involves precise detection of previous hospital admissions. The physician will often discover that the mother has taken the child to various hospitals and doctors in an attempt to offset or negate any suspicions of parental abuse. There is usually complete denial of any knowledge of inflicted trauma to the child, and more often, the attitude of complete innocence is transmitted to the examining physician or social service authorities. Difficulty in obtaining any type of history is often encountered, and diagnosis is dependent on the physical examination, x-ray findings and the high index of suspicion on the part of the physician.

There are many factors which unfavorably affect the normal

24

infant-adult relationship leading to the maltreatment syndrome. Among the more important and more frequently reported are a history of family discord, financial stress, alcoholism, illegitimacy, poverty, perversive tendencies, drug addiction and involvement with law enforcement agencies. Various grades of physical, mental and social retardation are encountered in many of these abusing parents. In some of these individuals obvious evidences of severe personality disorders have also been noted. Environmental stresses and strains related to life in the ghettos may serve as triggers resulting in incidents of child abuse in the lower socioeconomic strata.

In recent years, there has been a 15 to 20 percent rise in the number of infants born with narcotics addiction. In New York City alone approximately 800 addicted infants are born to addicted mothers each year. This rise is significant and may well attribute to the increased number of abused and neglected infants. The pediatrician should therefore be aware that this sizable number of infants is prone to neglect and oftentimes abuse by their addicted mothers. The infant of an addicted mother invites rejection and therefore should be protected and removed if necessary from the drug-addicted parent. The safety and welfare of this type of newborn should be uppermost in the physicians mind with consideration also given to helping the addicted parents, if at all possible, by referral to the appropriate agency.

The Massachusetts Society for the Prevention of Cruelty to Children studied causes of maltreatment in children in 1960. Data was available on 115 families with 180 children. It was concluded that these families had had problems at the time of marriage, and by the time the incidence of child abuse occurred, these problems had multiplied and intensified.

In a recent study by the Children's Division of The American Humane Association, a study of family characteristics was undertaken in a group of 328 cases of child abuse. It was noted that in almost two thirds of the situations, both parents were found to be living in the home. Of the one parent homes, just under 2 percent were homes where children lived with the father only. Mothers were the only parent in almost 10 percent of the cases. Family dislocation in a one parent home usually resulted from desertion, divorce, separation, hospitalization or imprisonment. Further study into the family problems of these cases of child abuse indicated that emotional immaturity was probably the greatest single cause for the destructive parental behavior.

Many of the parents involved in the inflicted abuse and maltreatment of children usually can be noted to react in complete reverse of normally accepted pattern of parental concern. They do not volunteer information to the physician, hospital authorities, social service workers or the law enforcement agencies. The individuals are usually evasive, often contradictory in their statements and often are irritated by the usual routine of medical questioning. Many of these parents give no indication of any obvious guilt or remorse for their actions of inflicted abuse. It has also been noted that some do not routinely visit the child in the hospital even when he is kept for weeks or even months. These parents are not concerned and do not question the discharge date. They are not willing to follow instructions concerning future clinic visits and the medical therapy prescribed. Many show surprisingly little reaction to social service investigations or to reporting to law enforcement agencies.

The character personality of the abusing parent need not show any outside signs of neurosis or psychosis; on the contrary, they may present the disarming attitude of overprotectiveness, cooperativeness and neatness in an attempt to mislead the physician or the social service worker. Social service workers reporting on cases encountered in our hospital have stated: "The mother's almost extreme cooperativeness, subtle lack of affect, rather compulsive neat personality and rather socially withdrawn behavior are similar to those described in other cases where physical abuse of children in the home was later proven."

Since many of these parents do give the outward impression of devoted parents, maltreatment is often overlooked by the physician and the syndrome is not considered in the differential diagnosis. This lack of awareness by the medical profession and the postponement of social service investigations often leads to future tragedy. Time must be considered of the essence in making a diagnosis and reporting such cases of maltreatment. Serious consequences for the child involved, for the parents and for other siblings may occur if too much time elapses between the admission of the child to the hospital and social service investigations leading to confirmation of the diagnosis. Once the diagnosis is established and reported, immediate attention must be directed toward the presence of other siblings in the family unit in order to protect them from future parental abuse.

Social service investigations have also revealed that usually one child in the family is selected and made the target for abuse and neglect, while the other siblings show evidence of overprotection. Often these abused and neglected children are made symbols of the parents expression of hostility to society based on a disapproved sexual and social pattern of existence. It is also interesting to note that some of these parents seem to have perceived and experienced their own parents as unloving, cruel and brutal. Authorities have indicated that this previous history of parental brutality has been evidenced in the parents now inflicting injury on their children as a retaliation expressed in their present behavior. It has been stated that the battering parent of today was the battered child of yesterday.

Duncan and his associates, in 1958, studied etiological factors in first degree murder. Studies by these physicians lead to the conclusion that among murderers, remorseless physical brutality at the hands of the parent had been a constant experience — brutality far beyond the ordinary excuses of discipline had been perpetrated upon them as children. It would seem that the absence of mature adult models to imitate and identify with, leads to the development of the same immature behavior which may result in physical abuse to other individuals and often leads to murder.

It must be admitted that these findings in the families of abused children are only impressions. They have been gathered on the basis of firsthand observations in addition to information volunteered by physicians, law enforcement officers, probation officers, child protective agencies and social service workers.

Perhaps the most important questions are what kind of parent it is that inflicts abuse and injury on a child; and what are the psychodynamics that are involved. It has been speculated that the abused child may in some way provoke an attack upon himself. The unwanted child, the sex of the child, his behavior and his health are characteristics that are presently under study as potential sources of child abuse in an abnormal, unhappy mother-child relationship.

Certain childrearing practices can lead to the development of a young adult who is characterized by antisocial behavior and by pervasive difficulty in functioning within acknowledged patterns of social acceptability. When a child is exposed to repeated episodes of violence, physical abuse, verbal abuse, neglect or rejection, the child oftentimes grows with anger and patterns his behavior on that of the model he has lived with during his childhood years.

It appears from available statistics that although the ratios of sex and race incidence did not change in the last decade, the average age of the abused victims increased significantly. The national analysis of official child neglect and abuse reports by the American Humane Society in 1978 clearly indicated that the victims of child maltreatment are older as well as younger children. Some adolescents are involved in some form of physical, sexual, as well as emotional, violence in their homes but are often inclined to cover up the parental abuse because of personal guilt or shame.

As professionals, we have concentrated our efforts on the "battered baby" and the maltreated young child and failed to continue our concern for the older child over twelve years who has tolerated his abuse into adolescence. An adolescent in an already multitroubled family is faced with personal problems of physical and sexual development and parental separation. Behavioral problems of an adolescent in a disrupted family unit cause the stressful situations that lead to adolescent abuse. In instances of adolescent abuse, there is a misalignment between a youth's "growing up" and a parent's "change of life" leaving both the parents and youth vulnerable to interfamilial violence. The maltreatment syndrome of children should therefore also encompass the teenager who is being increasingly recognized and reported as a victim of abuse, particularly in the areas of sexual exploitation. Many abused adolescents tend to escape from their maltreatment by leaving the family unit only to find societal abuse and neglect being inflicted upon them as "runaways" and the "throwaway" children of our society.

There have been a lack of medical and social services available to the abused and neglected teenager with resultant increases in the incidence of teenage pregnancies, juvenile delinquency, drug addiction, alcoholism and adolescent sexual exploitation and pornography. The development of services responsive to the needs of maltreated adolescents should be recognized and implemented by professionals dealing with the problem of child maltreatment.

In evaluating cases of child abuse and neglect at the New York Foundling Hospital Center for Parent and Child Development, it was found that the maltreated child is usually the victim of emotionally crippled parents who have had unfortunate circumstances surrounding their own childhood. The abusive parent appears to react to his own child as a result of past personal experiences of loneliness, lack of protection and love. Some of these parents have been raised by a variety of foster parents during their own childhood. The parents are unable to react normally to the needs of their own children.

The abusing parent frequently has a history of having been brutalized as a child himself and so perpetuates the pattern of violent behavior from generation to generation. This parent is unable to distinguish between his own childhood suffering and his vicious reactions toward his children. He is usually immature, narcissistic, demanding, impulsive, depressed and aggressive. He appears unwilling to accept responsibility as a parent. It seems he has a distorted perception of a particular child at a particular stage in its development. When the child is not able to perform, the parent may be triggered into a reaction leading to inflicted abuse.

Divorce, alcoholism, drug addiction, mental retardation, recurring mental illness, unemployment and financial stress are important factors often present in the family structure of abusing parents. These stress factors all play major roles in leading the potentially abusive parent to strike out at a particular child during a crisis situation. The three components, namely, a potentially abusing parent, a child and a sudden crisis are the necessary ingredients that give rise to child abuse and battering.

Abuse and neglect may be present when several of the following factors are in evidence:

The child seems unduly afraid of his parents.

The child is unusually fearful generally.

The child is kept confined, as in a crib or playpen (or cage), for overlong periods of time.

The child shows evidence of repeated skin or other injuries.

The child's injuries are inappropriately treated in terms of bandages and medication.

The child appears to be undernourished.

The child is given inappropriate food, drink or medicine.

The child is dressed inappropriately for weather conditions.

The child shows evidence of overall poor care.

The child cries often.

The child is described as "different" or "bad" by the parents.

The child does indeed seem "different" in physical or emotional makeup.

The child takes over the role of parent and tries to be protective or otherwise take care of the parent's needs.

The child is notably destructive and aggressive.

The child is notably passive and withdrawn.

The parent or parents discourage social contact.

The parent seems to be very much alone and to have no one to call upon when the stresses of parenthood get to be overwhelming.

The parent is unable to open up and share problems with an

interested listener and appears to trust nobody.

The parent makes no attempt to explain the child's most obvious injuries or offers absurd, contradictory explanations.

The parent seems to be quite detached from the child's problems.

The parent reveals inappropriate awareness of the seriousness of the child's condition (of the injury or neglect) and concentrates on complaining about irrelevant problems unrelated to the injured/neglected appearance of the child.

The parent blames a sibling or third party for the child's injury.

The parent shows signs of lack of control or fear of losing control.

The parent delays in taking the child in for medical care, either in case of injury or illness, or for routine checkups.

The parent appears to be misusing drugs or alcohol.

The parent ignores the child's crying or reacts with extreme impatience.

The parent has unrealistic expectations of the child: that he should be mature beyond his years; that he should "mother" the parent.

The parent indicates in the course of the conversation that he/she was reared in a motherless, unloving atmosphere; that he or she was neglected or abused as a child; that he or she grew up under conditions of harsh discipline and feels that it is right to impose those same conditions on his or her own children.

The parent appears to be of borderline intelligence, psychotic, or psychopathic. (Most laypersons will find it difficult to make a judgment here. It might be better for the observer to note whether the parent exhibits the minimal intellectual equipment to bring up a child; whether the parent is generally rational or irrational in manner; whether the parent is cruel, sadistic, and lacking remorse for hurtful actions.)

In summary, some of the characteristics of abusive parents include impulsivity, dependency, age inappropriateness, sadomasochism, egocentricity and narcissism. Abusive parents are demanding, isolated, depressed, angry and lacking self-esteem and self-control.

7

PREVENTIVE MEASURES

MEDICAL RESPONSIBILITIES

THE incidence of the maltreatment syndrome in children is startling. It is obviously a problem of increasing importance calling for the full cooperative resources and efforts of the medical, social and legal organizations of this country.

Various reports from child protective agencies reveal that less than one third of the child abuse cases seen by a physician are reported to law enforcement or social service agencies available in the community. This defect lies in the fact that the physician is unaware that parents can and often do willfully inflict serious damage to their children or even kill them. The physician is often reluctant to report a case of child abuse in his practice or hospital duty, since it may involve entanglement in legal matters and hours away from his medical chores. There is a definite lack in medical education concerning the maltreatment syndrome in children.

Presently, stimulated by the recent reports on this pediatric problem of serious import, the educational process of bringing this syndrome to the attention of the medical student, the hospital trainee and the practicing physician has begun. This process of education will challenge the reluctance of pediatricians and orthopedists to interpret parental neglect as the cause of inflicted trauma in children. Multiple fractures in various stages of resolution, dislocations, subdural hematoma, purpuric lesions of the skin, severe burns, unexplained malnutrition and failure to thrive should all be reasons for suspect by the alert physician.

Society is seeing evidence of parents who strike out against their children being reported in every day newspaper accounts. The medical profession is now faced with a greater number of reported injuries to children, resulting from beatings, burn

33

wounds, drownings, strangulations, suffocations and stabbings.

These inflicted abuses on children result in head and internal injuries that are responsible for the great many fatalities noted in this syndrome. The moral responsibility of the examining physician is to the maltreated child; he must be cognizant of the fact that over 50 percent of these children are liable to secondary injuries or death if appropriate steps are not taken to remove this child.

Holter and Friedman have indicated that approximately 10 percent of all children under six years of age routinely treated for accidents may have sustained their trauma by being physically abused. In another 10 percent, the accident is probably related to gross neglect. The physician should be aware that the incidence of suspected abuse rises to one out of three children if those seen for lacerations or ingestion of a drug or toxic substance are eliminated.

The physician is not fulfilling his responsibility if he remains out of the picture when human lives are involved. He must also be aware that for every abused child who enters the hospital there must be hundreds not seeking or receiving medical care.

The physician in practice should refer suspected cases involving maltreatment in children to the hospital for thorough diagnostic medical study and social investigations. If hospitalization of the child is not practical, the physician should report the case to the child protective society in his community or to the law enforcement agency, who in turn will take appropriate action to protect the child. If the physician is a house officer on duty in a hospital facility and suspects child abuse, the child should be admitted overnight whether or not the severity of the injury warrants it. This will give the physician the opportunity to ask the hospital social worker to see the parents and take another history. The house officer and social worker can then report their findings to the director of the medical service or a child abuse expert in the hospital who then decides whether or not to report the case to the child protective agencies. The final diagnosis of child abuse should involve the expert knowledge of an experienced physician and social worker.

Whenever necessary, the physician must testify as an expert witness interpreting his medical findings and answering questions relating to the specific inflicted abuse and injury. The physician must recognize the obvious neglect and physical abuse of children with a realistic approach and not reject the concept that parents can, and do, severely harm their children physically. He must be prepared to make specific diagnosis and recommendations which will result in protective measures for the maltreated child. Treatment of the child's injuries must be followed by immediate reporting of the abuse to the appropriate agencies who will investigate the child's home and family situation.

The medical societies are reappraising their approach to this difficult problem and must disseminate information to the physicians concerning this preventable syndrome. The medical societies should objectively indicate measures that the physician can take to protect the child from further abuse and trauma. This problem of parental delinquency resulting in child abuse has become a topic of top priority discussed at medical meetings at a state, regional and national level. The doctors' increased interest and recognition of the maltreatment syndrome in children, in addition to the well-substantiated significance of roentgenological findings, should lead to more case reporting and hopefully prevent child abuse, neglect, injury and death.

Every physician who has under his charge or care any child suspected of having wounds, fractures, dislocations or burns due to willfully inflicted injury, should report his findings to the child protective agency or the local law enforcement bureau in the community. Photographs of the child after admission to the hospital will greatly assist in confirming and documenting lesions due to abuse when they are related to the law enforcement agencies of the courts. Difficulties arise during court procedures when the abused child is presented in perfect health after a period of hospitalization and convalescence. The court in such cases may find it difficult to justify removal of the child from the mother under the presenting circumstances of physical well-being and holding to the concept of "mother belongs to child" and "child belongs to mother."

The following index of suspicion may be helpful to the physician before reporting cases of maltreatment:

History

1. Characteristic age — usually under three years.
2. General health of child — indicative of neglect.
3. Characteristic distribution of fractures.
4. Disproportionate amounts of soft tissue injury.
5. Evidence that injuries occurred at different times, with lesions in various stages of resolution.
6. Cause of recent trauma not known.
7. Previous history of similar episodes and multiple visits to various hospitals.
8. Date of injury prior to admission to hospital — delay in seeking medical help.
9. Child brought to hospital for complaint other than one associated with abuse and/or neglect, e.g. cold, headache, stomachaches, etc.
10. Reluctance of parents or caretakers to give information.
11. History related by parents or caretaker is usually at complete variance with the clinical picture and the physical findings noted on examinations of the child.
12. Parents' inappropriate reaction to severity of injury.
13. Family discord or financial stress, alcoholism, psychosis, drug addiction and inconsistent social history that varies according to intake worker.

Physical Examination

1. Signs of general neglect, failure to thrive, poor skin hygiene, malnutrition, withdrawal, irritability, repressed personality.
2. Bruises, abrasions, burns, soft tissue swellings, bites, hematomas, ocular damage, old healed lesions.
3. Evidences of dislocation and/or fractures of the extremities.
4. Unexplained symptoms of an acute abdomen — ruptured

viscera.
5. Neurologic findings associated with brain damage.
6. Coma, convulsions, death.
7. Symptoms of drug withdrawal or drug intoxication.

Differential Diagnosis

1. Scurvy and rickets.
2. Infantile cortical hyperostosis.
3. Syphilis of infancy.
4. Osteogenesis imperfecta.
5. Neurologic, organic brain damage.
6. Accidental trauma.

Radiologic Manifestations

1. Subperiosteal hemorrhages.
2. Epiphyseal separations.
3. Periosteal shearing.
4. Metaphyseal fragmentation.
5. Previously healed periosteal calcifications.
6. "Squaring" of the metaphysis.

After the physician has decided to report a case of child abuse, he should explain to the parents the medical findings. It should be made clear that these findings of suspected abuse of the child are being reported to the child protective agency in an effort to protect the child from further injury. In reporting the medical findings, the physician should be cautious and make definite efforts not to accuse any individual of the inflicted trauma until all the evidence is at hand. Parents may be suspected but should never be accused. Parents should be made aware of the situation and offered assistance in resolving the problems within the family that may have led to the maltreatment syndrome. The physician may, with justification, be angered by the battering parents but withholding such hostility will oftentimes contribute to the future protection of the child and other siblings.

An empathetic, nonjudgmental, objective physician dealing

with the maltreated child can affect the beginning of change in the parent-child relationship by showing parent-directed concern while questioning the parents.

The physician should begin by telling the parents that under the requirements of the law, a formal report must be filed of any injury to a child that is not clearly explained. It must be explained to the parents that this is a means of securing help and supportive family services to assist them in solving their problems. The physician should alleviate feelings of criminal court trials and hearings as a follow-up of the report. When properly approached, many parents will sense a feeling of relief when informed of possible assistance and intervention. The reporting process should be aimed at helping the multitroubled family, not at intensifying an existing explosive family situation.

The physician's first responsibility is to the child, encouraging immediate removal of the child from a life-threatening environment if necessary. Once the child has been treated and protected from further abuse, the physician and social worker can then turn their attention to the parents. In most instances, the child protective agencies will assume responsibility for the complete evaluation and disposition of the child to its own home under supervision, to the courts, to a child caring institution or to a foster home. It cannot be overemphasized that the problem demands the most delicate handling by all involved disciplines; nevertheless, the physician's intervention is urgent if the child is to be saved and protected from further abuse. The physician who is reluctant to report or does not want to become involved in cases of suspected child abuse and battering, aids and abets those guilty of maltreating children. The American physician can no longer legally remain silent under presently existing mandatory reporting laws in all fifty of the states and the District of Columbia.

A physician's responsibilities in the problem of child abuse can be encouraged by the formation of a child abuse committee. This committee, officially designated by hospital authorities, would review all child abuse cases and make specific recommendations as to the social, medical and legal measures needed for the protection of the maltreated child. A committee of this type should have a multidisciplinary team, including a physician as chairman, a social worker, a hospital administrator and a psychiatrist.

Kempe has proposed the development of regional metropolitan centers for the study and care of abused and neglected children. Within these centers, experienced professionals would evaluate methods of early case finding, develop means to identify the family that can be strengthened, coordinate community services and protect children from physical abuse. In addition, a center of this type could evaluate current methods of care of the abused child and his parents and provide the impetus for new therapeutic approaches.

Hospital sponsored seminars on child abuse can provide interns and residents in all departments with information necessary to implement child abuse laws. Educational programs sponsored by the medical societies will orient practicing physicians to the problem and also disseminate information to the medical, social and legal disciplines involved with child abuse.

The law is definite as to who should report, stating "any physician, surgeon, dentist, osteopath, optometrist, chiropractor, podiatrist, resident, intern, registered nurse or Christian Science practitioner having reasonable cause to suspect that a child is an abused or neglected child shall report or cause reports to be made." The concept of broadening the class of persons required to report beyond physicians has gained considerable support in recent years.

The physician must bear in mind that he need have only reasonable cause to suspect. He need make no definitive decision and is not required to make any accusation as to who caused the suspected injuries. It is important to note here that the law specifically protects the reporting person against any civil or criminal proceedings resulting from such reporting when made in good faith.

In summary: The physician's responsibility in suspected cases of child abuse and neglect should include the following steps.

1. Making the diagnosis of the maltreatment syndrome.

2. Immediate intervention and admission of the child to the hospital.
3. Complete assessment — medical history, physical examination, skeletal survey, colored photographs of injuries.
4. Report case to the appropriate community Department of Social Service or Child Protective Unit responsible for investigation.
5. During hospitalization of child, request social worker investigation and report.
6. Conference within seventy-two hours with members of the Hospital's Child Abuse Committee.
7. Arrange referral to program of care for child and parent with multidisciplinary staff.

SOCIAL RESPONSIBILITIES

Child Protective Agencies and Social Service

The Children's Division of the American Humane Association has for years been a leader in the movement to provoke interest in the field of child protection. They have made a real effort to awaken communities to their responsibility toward neglected children. The Children's Division has stimulated and promoted positive action in the direction of coordinating community resources to plan a better program which will result in bringing real assistance to the children and families involved in this vital problem. More recently, the United States National Center on Child Abuse and Neglect has provided a national focus for efforts to prevent and treat child abuse and neglect. The current wave of concern over the rising tide of childhood neglect and abuse is resulting in a closer and more finite examination of the existing methods and techniques for helping these children and their families.

More active casework techniques must be established which will reach out toward the neglecting parents and abused child. Only through a complete social service approach can the evidence that is presented by the medical profession be utilized to the utmost in bringing about the removal of these parents from a grossly inadequate situation into a more responsible position.

The social service agencies throughout the country play a very important part in helping the countless number of disturbed parents who strike out against society and the world through this abnormal behavior of aggression toward the child. These social agencies must be prepared to treat family problems which bring about this neglect. They must be prepared to eliminate many of the conditions and factors in the environment that motivate this type of parental delinquency.

The Children's Division of the American Humane Association undertook a survey late in the fall of 1964 to assess and evaluate the status and extent of child protective services across the nation. Among other facts, it was noted that there was a growing awareness that in too many communities too little was being done toward well-orientated casework service dealing with the protection of children. There seemed to be a lack of knowledge or understanding of the basic and fundamental concepts as developed by the practitioners in the field of child protection. There was also a lack of child protective agencies in certain communities.

Child protection (and the agencies organized for this purpose) was first stimulated by the public protest and concern over the treatment of little Mary Ellen, a child who was maltreated in New York City in 1874.

In the beginning, these child protective agencies exerted law enforcement and emphasized the removal of the abused child and punishment of the offending parents. Little scientific or social interest was evident during the early years of the child protective agencies. With the passing of time, society has become aware that with many sociomedical problems preventive measures foster the betterment of society and avoid the complications of disease. Many leaders in the child protective agencies have recently emphasized the importance of prevention and have fought against using prosecution and legal action as a means of treating parental delinquents. Law enforcement is being correlated with precise and complete casework. There is now a state of transition; there is an advance from the strict isolated social investigation to the study of social and medical aspects of certain problems involving parental or juvenile delinquency. This integration has been slow but is being greatly influenced by the rapid growth of the medicosocial techniques used in evaluating certain types of social behavior and disease.

The Children's Division of the American Humane Association states: "In many sections of the country excellent planning makes provision for a wide range of welfare services and activities in a voluntary board management and control, or in the public auspices such as county, state or federal government. These make available to the community the family patterns of health services, family counseling, child welfare services, recreation facilities and public assistance. More specifically they provide financial assistance to families; financial and other aid to mothers and children; clinical aid with respect to health problems; psychological and psychiatric consultation and treatment; advice on family problems and marital difficulties; day care for children, foster home care, adoptions and institutional services." They also have stated, rightfully and most emphatically, that these are services which are open to any one who needs them and asks for them.

Therein lies, probably, the true nature of this entire problem of parental delinquency. Parents who neglect their children do not ask for these services; if they did their children would not be neglected. It is therefore the responsibility of social service agencies and child protective agencies throughout the country to seek out these parents through case findings and case investigation. Attempts must be made to bring the parent to the protective agency and rehabilitate him with guidance and counseling on the fundamental obligations of parenthood. If this is not done, agencies that have been organized for the protection of children and society may just as well be nonexistent. Their effectiveness can only be measured by the contact they make with those who are in need of the service.

The New York State Youth Commission, several years ago, in attempting to define the rights of all children, stated in clear terms what they have called:

THE CHILDREN'S BILL OF RIGHTS

For each child, regardless of race, color or creed:

1. The right to the affection and intelligent guidance of understanding parents.
2. The right to be raised in a decent home in which he or she is adequately fed, clothed, and sheltered.
3. The rights to the benefits of religious guidance and training.
4. The right to a school program which in addition to sound academic training offers maximum opportunity for individual development and preparation for living.
5. The right to receive constructive discipline for the proper development of good character, conduct and habits.
6. The right to be secure in his or her community against all influence detrimental to proper and wholesome development.
7. The right to individual selection of free and wholesome recreation.
8. The right to live in a community in which adults practice the belief that the welfare of their children is of primary importance.
9. The right to receive good adult example.
10. The right to a job commensurate with his or her ability, training and experience, and protection against physical or moral employment hazards which adversely affect wholesome development.
11. The right to early diagnosis and treatment of physical handicap and mental and social maladjustments at public expense whenever necessary.

This bill of rights not only enumerates the rights of children, but also indicates the obligations and the responsibilities of society and of all parents. It is an intimate part of the social service worker in rendering the best possible case investigation. The neglected and abused child becomes a ward of the social service worker or child protective agency under this bill of rights, until the threatening factors in the child's environment are removed.

It is the responsibility of the social service worker to foster through contact, investigation and understanding the rights of children and the duties and obligations of parents to their children. It is through the recognition of these mutual rights that family relationships become healthier. This in turn results in the removal of factors responsible for the inflicted neglect and abuse of children found in present-day society.

The social service obligations begin with thorough investigation and precise casework. They also refer the case to the necessary agencies which will provide financial aid, foster care, institutional care, homemakers, lay therapists or adoptive services if such are indicated. The child protective agency can only begin action or begin investigation into a case of child mistreatment after being informed either by the school authorities, law enforcement agencies, social agencies, the courts or the community. For this reason, society must be aroused; it must be well-informed concerning all aspects of this disease that causes countless numbers of children to be either battered, crippled for life or killed.

The child protective agency has vested authority which has been conferred upon it either by the law, as in the case of a Society for the Prevention of Cruelty to Children or a public or governmental agency specifically charged and empowered with such responsibility and authority, or the authority may come from a community assent which implies that public opinion has given the agency the right to intervene to protect these children.

To punish the juvenile has not been the answer to the problem of delinquency, as has been noted from past experience, nor does punishing parents who have neglected or abused their children bring any real help to the parents or assistance to the child. The abusing parental delinquent or the individual inflicting trauma on a helpless child must be assisted sociologically, psychiatrically and medically to construct the type of personality which will eliminate the neglect and abuse so inflicted upon children. These personality disorders which are found in many of these abusive parents, including immaturity, mental deficiency and other physical, mental, emotional and moral inadequacies, must be exposed and treated by appropriate means in order to treat the true cause of this disease and not just the symptoms. These victims of modern frustrations and antisocial living, triggered by economic and environmental, moral and emotional tensions, must receive the necessary help to make them better citizens and better parents. One source of help may be to provide a homemaker. This individual can serve as a lay therapist, can serve as a maternal figure to "mother" the mother, and can assist the immature mother in childrearing and housekeeping practices.

The social service agencies and the child protective agencies, therefore, must probe into the causative agents responsible for this type of parental behavior which leads to the maltreatment syndrome in children. They must become leaders in the research efforts that must be directed to study the type of parent who will abuse, neglect and even kill his own children. They must also study the type of child that becomes the victim of the abusive parent or individual. They must practice the ways and means of preventing this type of antisocial behavior in modern society. All these studies and investigations by social service agencies throughout the country should receive the support of city, state and national authorities, in order that their work might help stem the tide of parental delinquency leading to further deterioration of society at large. The world community and all peoples, especially those who are in positions to offer assistance, must accept this challenge. Those who have been trained in case study must set forth a new and more comfortable pattern of living for these unfortunate individuals. Only in this way can we fulfill our obligations to future generations — the children of today.

A most complete list of child protective services in every state of the United States has been compiled by Vincent De Francis, Director of the Children's Division of The American Human Association and should serve all those interested in the problem of the maltreatment of children. This very comprehensive report can be secured from the Children's Division of The American Humane Association, Post Office Box 1266, Denver, Colorado. Vincent De Francis has been most concerned and interested in this problem and has contributed a great amount of information on protective services, child welfare work and the community interpretation of the specialized role and function of the child protective agency. He has stated that there is no other area of social work activity that has been so little understood as that of child protection. No other area of social work practices required as long to gain status and recognition. De Francis has stimulated and proposed a dramatic change in philosophy toward more aggressive casework in this field of child protection.

The community must face up to the responsibility that the maltreatment of children is a true problem of increasing incidence and importance. The communities throughout the country must establish services which will protect the child and rehabilitate the parents when physical, financial and emotional problems make them unable to cope with the stresses and strains of everyday living. Communities cannot afford to further neglect this all-important problem involving the parents of today and the future parents of tomorrow. The physical, moral, spiritual and emotional status of America's future generation depends on the action of society toward this problem of maltreatment today. This is a preventive program which must be carried out immediately in order to prevent further deterioration, destruction and breakdown of our present day social and moral system.

Since the first case of recorded child maltreatment in 1874, very little has been done medically, socially and legally toward the prevention of child abuse, when compared with the incidence and the worldwide existence of this problem. Why has it taken all these years to arouse public opinion or arouse the state legislatures throughout the country to pass a series of laws protecting the rights of children and authorizing the creation of societies and social service agencies for the prevention of cruelty to children? These are questions that must be answered by each member of society.

Leaders in the field of child protection must grow; they must communicate and bring about necessary application of preventive and protective measures which will result in a safer, more complete and more productive society. A neglected child is, and must be, the concern of the entire community. The community must cooperate with the child protective agencies in existence; the child protective agencies in turn must integrate their efforts and studies with the medical-legal aspects of the problem. The power of the child protective agency therefore depends on its being alerted by the community and its coordination with the medical and legal sections of our society.

In the publication "Community Cooperation for Better Child Protection" by Vincent De Francis, child protection is defined as

A specialized case work service on behalf of children who are neglected, abused, exploited or cruelly treated. It recognizes that neglect usually results where parents, unable to function adequately because of inability to cope with their own problems, fail to meet the basic physical, medical or emotional needs of their children. The focus of the service is preventive and impunitive and is geared toward a rehabilitation of the home and a treatment of the motivating factors which underlie the neglect. This implies that parents and children are given help with those problems which have directly affected the parents' ability to provide proper care and service. The service is usually initiated on a complaint or referral from sources outside the family. The agency providing protective services has authority granted it by law or a charter which imposes an obligation to provide the service when needed and which grants the right to explore and study and evaluate the facts of neglect and their effect on children. The agency has responsibility for invoking the authority of the juvenile court with such action as is necessary to secure adequate protection, care and treatment of children whose parents are unable or unwilling to use the help offered by the agency.

The child protective agencies can meet their obligations and responsibilities only if they receive the community's cooperation which it is organized to serve. The community must recognize the problem of child abuse and neglect. It can no longer afford to have blind spots concerning the problems of parental delinquency as they have in the past concerning the problem of juvenile delinquency. The community must give personal and financial assistance to the child protective agencies. Without the full cooperation of city, county and state organizations, child protective agencies cannot operate. The recognition by the community and state authorities of this all important problem will result in helping the child protective agencies meet the basic needs necessary to protect the child and parents involved in the maltreatment syndrome.

Child protective programs must be organized where they are not available. Appropriate administrative structures with authority must be supported through adequate financial budgets. The community must remove the dilemma that now exists in society resulting from society's unwillingness to accept and acknowledge this most important problem of child abuse and neglect. Community resources are the fuel with which the child protective agencies operate. The community and every member of society can truly protect and prevent a child from being a victim of abuse and neglect by providing necessary support to the child protective programs in his area. The effectiveness of any child protective agency and the results that it produces runs parallel with the support it receives from the community.

At the present time, child protection in many states is entirely carried by such voluntary agencies as the Society for the Prevention of Cruelty to Children, Children's Aid Societies and Humane Societies. With the enactment of Title Five of the Social Security Act, public child welfare agencies have increasingly accepted responsibility for the protection of children. In many states, special child protective units are set up in the county public child welfare service. The community cannot neglect its responsibility in establishing necessary health and social welfare programs which will support family life, provide opportunities for children who are in need, and improve conditions which affect children adversely. With the establishment of these organizations, eradication of social ills will become a reality, and through the combined efforts of these community forces all of society will benefit.

In summary: There must be an acknowledgment by society, immediately, that the problem of child abuse and neglect does exist and is on the increase. Recognition of this syndrome as an index of social and parental delinquency should stimulate community cooperation through the establishment, if not already in existence, of organizations, protective agencies and courts for better child protection. These societies should be given the utmost financial support in order to establish agencies with authoritative administrative structures of the highest caliber throughout the country.

The social service workers play an all-important role in the integration of the medical, legal and social aspects of the maltreatment of children. These individuals must be well-trained in investigation and case finding. It is their responsibility for planning and presenting the social and medical findings of the case to the court authorities. The social service personnel cooperate and assist the medical group in identifying any existing destructive drives within the family unit and thereby afford protection of the child from further traumatic experiences. The social and medical members of this team must enable the parents to accept and receive psychiatric help, if indicated, thereby strengthening family understandings and protecting the parents from future consequences of abnormal social behavior. It is most important that there be a realistic coordination of efforts and communication of ideas between the competent social worker with special skills and the physician or agent reporting the child abuse case. Only in this way can protective services function and carry out their responsibility to the child and parents with the appropriate therapeutic services available.

Responsibilities of the community in the social structure of the United States therefore include the social service investigation of suspected cases of child abuse, education and rehabilitation of parental delinquents and the cooperative integrated efforts of all social agencies, on a local, state and federal level, in combating the problem of maltreatment in children.

PREVENTION OF CHILD ABUSE

The community and the child care agencies have several responsibilities in the field of child maltreatment, namely, the identification and diagnosis of child maltreatment; the provision of a therapeutic multidisciplinary, human support system; and an educational program that will not only insure public awareness but provide the professionals and paraprofessionals with the necessary information that will allow the fulfillment of their responsibilities in the identification, diagnosis and treatment of child abuse. Primary prevention is also an important responsibility of the community. In this area, the social, medical and legal disciplines must offer their resources and work collectively in order to more effectively control the rising incidence of child abuse. To achieve any success in the area of prevention, massive programs on parenting and family care must be developed and implemented. Other efforts that can provide effective preventive services include:

1. The establishment of "hot lines" or "lifelines" such as the organization called CALM (Child Abuse Listening Mediation), started in 1970. The CALM hot line functions as a crisis intervention service which provides the distressed, potentially abusive parent with an immediate outlet with someone to talk to. This type of crisis intervention can oftentimes prevent a parent from striking out at a child during a time of crisis. This service to the parent also provides a means of identifying parents in need of help so that referrals can be made to appropriate community family services. In many areas of the country, these crisis intervention hot lines are manned by volunteers who are nonprofessional. However, if at all possible, administration of these hot lines by professionals should provide information of immediate help to the caller.

2. "Volunteers" have in the past provided a source of important contributions in the field of child welfare. In the last decade, they have become involved and supplemented service staffs of child abuse prevention and treatment efforts. In this area, they have proven to be effective in direct services to clients ranging from answering "hot lines" to working directly with abusive parents as lay therapists. A variety of volunteer responsibilities in child abuse and neglect programs have been developed in recent years and have been used successfully in the interdisciplinary approach to intervention and therapy.

   Trained volunteers are important assets in any program dealing with abusive parents and their children. The basic requirements for paraprofessional volunteerism include a maturity developed through having lived and survived difficult life experiences, emotional stability, nonjudgmental warmth, empathy, patience, honesty and a basic capacity of caring and a willingness to give time and concern in helping others.

Volunteers have proven .their effectiveness in a variety of responsibilities including: Parent Aides (SCAN); crisis hot lines (Parental Stress Services), self-help groups (Parents' Anonymous), surrogate parents, lay therapists (shelter treatment homes and outpatient programs); day care centers, therapeutic nurseries, and crisis family centers; child advocacy groups (Citizens' Committees and Task Forces); medical and legal services to families; education and public awareness campaigns; fund raising for child abuse treatment and prevention programs.

3. Teach parenting within the school system. Establish a curriculum that will allow young people in elementary and high schools to learn the responsibilities of parenting. Courses in child abuse should be included to allow students who have been abused to recognize their potential for violence and thereby seek preventive professional assistance. Providing educational parenting experiences to young people will help to reestablish the stability of the family unit.

Within the community, formal adult training courses for parenting are almost nonexistent. This is one of the biggest deficits at the present time since we are offering minimal experience or training in how to be a parent. Parent effectiveness training programs such as P.E.T. provide adult education in the skills of parenting. The P.E.T. program was established by Dr. Thomas Gordon and has been found effective in this area of providing parents with important information. The need to provide parents with this information is important in developing good parent-child relationships. These healthy experiences and expressions of good parenting can prevent some of the traumatic crisis situations which trigger child abuse in the family unit.

Another major area of prevention lies in sex education

beyond the physical-sexual level — a human sexuality curriculum that includes and emphasizes the understanding of family life skills and the long-term effects and responsibilities of child rearing.

Teenagers must be made aware that having sex is filled with emotional, physical and social consequences. Sex education in the schools should therefore include such things as family values, a healthy acceptance of the responsibilities that go with sexuality, emotional stability in marital relationships and a willingness to accept the consequences of one's actions. This kind of comprehensive education in human sexuality can meet the real developmental needs of teenagers searching for their sexual identity and the responsibilities that go with becoming a parent. Lest we forget the other parent, namely the father, let us remember that parenthood is a mutual responsibility and so all efforts must be made to provide supportive services to the teenage father as well. Increasingly more involvement of the father is being mandated by law.

4. The concept of a "health visitor" to act as a primary health screener for entire families is another positive effort in primary prevention. The health visitor as proposed by Dr. C. Henry Kempe would provide an assessment of the parent-child relationships; advise on common well-child problems; provide a liaison with available health community resources; and screen for childhood developmental abnormalities. The health visitor would initiate regular visits with the young mother soon after her discharge with her baby from the hospital. This intervention would provide primary preventive measures to a parent in a nonthreatening manner and establish a strong link between the private and public health care system of our communities.

This type of early intervention as proposed by Dr. Kempe would substantially add to the hopes of reducing the incidence of child maltreatment. A good plan would be one that would have periodic visitation to families by professionals or paraprofessionals that would offer help before the occurrence of a crisis situation. This is about the best type of preventive pediatrics available today. Implementation of a friendly visitor program within communities can serve as an important and effective therapeutic modality. Parent aides and homemakers such as those in the Parent Aide program (which was first developed in Denver by Dr. Kempe and his associates) can also help and serve parents who are in stressful situations thereby prevent them from becoming involved in crisis situations leading to neglect and abuse.

All of these home health care services emphasize prevention designed to have children remain at home with their families. The nurse, social worker or paraprofessional visiting the home provides an early periodic screening program for the detection of child maltreatment. This "helper" should be able to give direct services within her or his own competency and be able to prescribe and help obtain needed services such as homemakers, home health aides and the variety of respite services for the parents and child that may be required. They should also be qualified to provide on-going practical information as well as counseling to the parents on all aspects of child rearing, child nutrition and effective parenting. Training of these professional and paraprofessional "family helpers" in the broad provision of these home health services is an essential first step in this preventive approach. The priorities for recipients of these preventive services should focus on parents, especially single parents with preschool or school-age children living at home.

5. Day Care Centers, Family Day Care Centers, Infant Day Care Centers and Crisis Nurseries may well be a means of providing families and children with the necessary human resources necessary to maintain family stability and, in many cases, prevent child abuse. These child care programs allow parents to obtain needed relief from the constant presence and pressures of children that can cause or trigger child abuse. Day Care programs can provide an educational experience for the child and a therapeutic

respite for the parents.

6. Mother-Child programs that provide support systems to the young mother in the development of a parent-child relationship. A model mother-child program developed at the New York Foundling Hospital in 1972 provides a residential setting and a variety of services enabling young mothers to grow into parents who can accept responsibility for themselves and their children. The program assists the young mother who wishes to keep her baby by providing her with a homelike atmosphere in a residence of the Foundling Hospital while being assisted in the development of parenting skills. During her stay in the residence, the mother is also given the opportunity to complete her education or receive some type of on-the-job training in an area which will assist her in developing skills that will help her secure future employment. The mother and child remain in the program from one year to eighteen months.

7. Screening for the high risk mothers during prenatal and postpartum periods offers an unique opportunity for preventive child maltreatment intervention. Immediate involvement with the parent by attending physicians, nurses, social workers and health visitors will help avoid the parental misbehavior that leads to child neglect, failure to thrive and physical injury to the child.

Although we are more aware of the psychodynamics of child abuse today, we are not as cognizant of the predictive parameters of the problem. It is obvious that if one could develop a predictive scale of potential child abusers and/or abnormal parenting experiences and practices, early effective intervention could be facilitated and thereby prevent damage to the victim, namely the newborn infant or child.

Drs. Henry Kempe and Jane Gray have recognized the importance of early detection during the prenatal and neonatal periods. These periods offer the observer an excellent opportunity to study the parents' attitudes, personality structure, social contacts, degree of intrafamilial communication, their values and their "hang ups." It also provides during the neonatal period an opportunity to assess the newborn infant's behavior, as well as parent-child interactions, parent-parent relationships and any indicator of potentially harmful child rearing patterns. Intervention during these critical sensitive and emotionally laden periods can prevent parent-induced damage to the child and allow providing the human network of support for the parents that will insure the child's fullest physical, emotional and intellectual potential for development.

Gray, Kempe and co-workers, utilizing an interview, a questionnaire and labor, delivery and postpartum observations, have established that perinatal assessment and simple intervention with mothers "high risk for abnormal parenting practices" significantly improves the infants' chances for escaping future physical injury.

Some "high risk" characteristics include a history of child abuse, adolescent pregnancy, financial problems, social isolation, alcoholism, drug addiction and inadequate child care arrangements.

Our concern for children must begin with the mother's pregnancy, her feelings about the pregnancy and her anxiety and fears during the prenatal period. This type of attention to the mother's needs plays an important role in supporting the necessary "mothering" that is essential during infancy to insure healthy child-rearing interactions between mother and child.

Although the newborn does not know or recognize his mother during the first weeks of life, the development of the child begins at this time and the months to follow. This phase in the developmental process is called the "imprinting stage": the time when a mother's smiling face, support, comfort and love and the pleasurable experience of nursing the newborn infant contribute to the secure tension-reducing experience of the child in an intimate relationship with his mother in which there is mutual satisfaction and enjoyment. This type of mother-child relationship produces a consistent, need-satisfying experience for the child that makes it possible for him to similarly respond in adult life.

Scientific appreciation of the neonate's remarkable capacities for social interaction have been documented by the works of Klaus and Kennell of Western Reserve University School of Medicine. The authors have emphasized the importance of early parent-infant bonding that can prevent both psychological and physical complications after childbirth.

Recent studies validate the importance of unrestricted interaction between parents and newborns during the "sensitive" first few hours after birth. Parents who had extended contact with their newborns immediately postpartum were found to have more extensive verbal interchange with their children two years later. Mothers whose contact with their newborns was increased beyond normal hospital contacts during the first thirty minutes postpartum were found three months later to spend more time fondling and kissing their babies than a control group of mothers who spend more time cleaning their babies.

Routine hospital policy of separation and minimal contact between mother and infant to prevent infection and manage physical problems may well interfere with early maternal affection and responsiveness presently being called maternal-infant bonding. Whether it is called "mothering," "bonding" or "parenting", there is no doubt that the earlier babies develop warm, secure and tender relationships with their parents, the better. Significant disruptions in early parent-child interaction creates a situation of risk for the child, particularly when the child is difficult to care for or the parent is under stress. The importance of parent-infant bonding in the prevention of child abuse has been reported by Margaret Lynch. She noted that when abused children were studied and compared with their not abused siblings, it was found that maternal-infant separations during the first six months were frequently noted. The separations were often due to an abnormal pregnancy, an abnormal delivery and illnesses in the child or mother during the first year.

It would appear that dysfunction of the family and the weaknesses of the family bonds are related to the traditional practice of separating mother and baby after birth and oftentimes excluding the husband during the labor, delivery and the postdelivery experiences. Therefore, the correct treatment of parents during pregnancy, delivery and the early infancy period may well be an important early preventive technique in helping eliminate child abuse.

Any real program aimed at helping to eliminate child abuse must begin with education and training of expectant parents. The programs of education should not be geared solely to the physical aspects of pregnancy and the birth of the baby, but should contain explanations of the emotional and psychological impact the pregnancy and the birth will have for the mother and the father — discussions of what pregnancy means to them, what the birth of the child and the nurturing of the infant and young child will mean to their own lifestyle. While a doctor or nurse can certainly handle the physical aspects of such an educational program, the discussions around the feelings of the participants should be led by a psychiatrist, a psychologist or a social worker. Such a team effort can only have positive results if conducted consistently and followed through after the baby's birth.

To many of our observations on child abuse are ex post facto. Could it have been prevented? If so, it has to begin with early identification, effective intervention and supportive education during and immediately after pregnancy.

Hospitals and doctors can facilitate the prevention of child maltreatment especially among the pregnant adolescent population by assessment of their antiquated policies and practices prenatally, during labor and delivery, and in the first days of life. This is exactly the time when the present system of medical care often does not provide the necessary professional help to these new young parents. Hospitals must develop their resources so that they can play an effective role. Efforts should be made by hospital personnel toward establishing routine prenatal assessment of the "high risk" or "at risk" potential of all families using existing indicators proposed by Gray and Kempe. A precise evaluation of the circumstances surrounding the pregnancy will provide information about the adolescent's own early childhood experiences, family and peer relationships, her feelings about herself and her pregnancy and her future plans for herself and her baby.

Significantly greater attention must be given to assessing the progress of parent-infant bonding beginning in the delivery room. Material rejecting behaviors can be easily identified by nurses and physicians in the delivery room. Such assessments should be handled as routine obstetrical practice. The active involvement and participation of the father in each stage of the prenatal care, in the delivery and in the nursery is an essential component in a preventive hospital program. The father should be permitted in the delivery room. In addition, efforts must be made to reappraise physical facilities to provide easy access of the mother to the infant and modify or change hospital nursery policies that separate the normal or sick newborn infants from their mothers. Hospitals and physicians must actively promote practices that will avoid separation of mother from her infant during the first twenty-four hours in order to enhance parent-infant bonding.

Other preventive services for the pregnant adolescent and teenage parent should include early detection of pregnancy and comprehensive prenatal care; the availability of good infant care combined with programs attended by the mother; protective services for adolescents and shelters for unwed teenagers offering legal, vocational and family planning instructions and guidance; and long-term follow-up services for a minimum of two years.

Summary

Improvements are necessary to make the delivery of child care services in this country more effective and appropriate, especially in dealing with the prenatal and postnatal care of "high risk" mothers. All urban or poor populations have an increased maternal and infant morbidity and mortality rate which is oftentimes coupled with inadequate medical preventive services and the attitudinal cultural barriers that impede the delivery of these services to the recipients. We must therefore develop child abuse preventive programs for the high risk population; the underprivileged; the handicapped, the drug addicted; the alcoholics; the woefully immature and the unwed single parents. The encouraged participation of these parents in early preventive programs that offer human support services will ensure that quality of life for child and parents that will not incite parental misbehavior.

There are several questions that must be answered if the problem of prevention in the field of child maltreatment is to be dealt with effectively. Are there adequate follow-up programs for children in early childhood development after birth to insure that parent and child of proper medical and social support? Are there early identification methods of detection of children in high risk categories such as the hyperactive, the psychotic or the handicapped, in order to offer speedy referral and treatment services?

Prevention is a community responsibility and one of the most effective means of alleviating child abuse in this country. Education, particularly for parents, will reduce the massive alienation of parents and children which causes family crisis, breakdown, intrafamilial violence and subsequent child abuse.

Single parent family projects should be developed in order to provide a place where single parents can share information, skills and support; where they can work with other parents with similar concerns or tragedies toward change and growth into the exciting challenge of responsible parenting.

TREATMENT OF CHILD ABUSE

Caring for the maltreating parents was in the past considered a social service responsibility and essentially the burden of the public and private social work agencies. However, traditional social work intervention in caring for these parents has not been totally effective. With the increased awareness and knowledge of why and how child maltreatment occurs, there has been an increased interest and involvement by other professionals and paraprofessionals in public and private social child-caring agencies, child protective societies and hospitals. A variety of innovative crisis intervention programs staffed by various disciplines with different techniques are providing effective therapeutic models. There is no evidence at present to indicate that any one therapeutic approach to the treatment of abusive parents is more effective than another for a select group of patients.

There are no easy answers to the problems of parenting, especially when dealing with the abusive or neglectful parent. Expertise and time are required to unravel the causative factors. Social and environmental factors may be found which, though objectively undesirable, are not necessarily responsible for the parent's malfunctioning; the adverse social factors may be the result of the parent's psychological state rather than the cause. If the physician lacks training, time and interest to ascertain which factors are responsible for the child abuse situation, an evaluation by a social worker, psychologist, psychiatric social worker or psychiatrist is essential. Without this type of data it is impossible to develop a rational program to prevent further abuse and neglect.

How can adequate parenting be obtained for the infant in the future? To achieve this goal two major intervention options exist: Efforts can be made to enable the parent to function more appropriately, or a permanent substitute parent can be provided through foster home placement. Several basic approaches can be used to improve the parents functioning:

1. Eliminate or diminish the social or environmental stresses.
2. Lessen the adverse psychological impact of the social fac-

tors on the parent.

3. Reduce the demands on the mother to a level which is within her capacity (this can be achieved through day care placement of the infant or provision of a housekeeper or baby sitter).
4. Provide emotional support, encouragement, sympathy, stimulation, instruction in maternal care, and aid in learning to plan for, assess, and meet the needs of the infant (supportive casework).
5. Resolve or diminish the inner psychic conflict (psychotherapy).

Ideally, each parent should have an intervention plan developed for her based upon an assessment of a number of factors which include:

1. The factors responsible for the parent's dysfunction.
2. The severity of the parent's psychopathology.
3. The overall prognosis for achieving adequate mothering.
4. Time estimated to achieve meaningful change in the mother's ability to mother.
5. Whether the parent's dysfunction is confined to this infant or involves all of her children.
6. The extent to which the mother's malfunctioning extends to her roles, i.e. wife, homemaker, housekeeper.
7. The extent to which the parent's overall malfunctioning, if this is the case, is acute or chronic (reflects a lifelong pattern).
8. The extent to which the mother's malfunctioning is confined to infants as opposed to older children.
9. The parent's willingness to participate in the intervention plan.
10. The availability of personnel and physical resources to implement the various intervention strategies.
11. The risk of the child's sustaining physical abuse by remaining in the home.

All of the above sounds most impersonal, yet it is all aimed at helping the persons involved in child abuse situations. No help can be given until the situation is recognized for what it is and brought to the attention of those who can help. It all comes down to rescuing the two individuals involved — the abusing parent and the child abused. The process of identifying and of rehabilitating these two important persons is a long process indeed.

Many programs have been developed throughout the country to try to do this very thing: rehabilitate mother and/or father and child. Dr. C. Henry Kempe, Chief Pediatrician at the University of Colorado Medical Center, was the trailblazer in setting up an innovative program to achieve rehabilitation.

One such program that has been in existence since 1972 is located at the New York Foundling Hospital Center for Parent and Child Development in New York City.

This program attempts to utilize the best treatment approaches known to date and, at the same time, to provide a residential treatment approach so as not to separate the child from the mother. This model program stresses (1) protection of the child without actual separation and (2) crisis management for the parent.

The advantages of the residential component are the following:

1. It is the only way to observe the interaction between parent and child twenty-four hours a day, seven days a week.
2. It is the best way to diagnose the severity of the problem.
3. It makes possible the formulation of a more realistic treatment plan.
4. It avoids the trauma of separation of child from parent.
5. It enables the parent to establish a meaningful relationship with the staff due to the regularity of contacts.

The treatment methods that are utilized in this program are:

1. Paraprofessionals who have been found to be effective in achieving positive results. These paraprofessionals are used in two positions:
   a. Group Mothers who provide the role model in assisting the abusing parent in caring for the child by instructing the mother in preparing meals, handling tan-

trums of children, responding to child's physical needs as well as emotional needs and providing human support to the mother in properly caring for her child as well as herself.

b. Social Service Assistants. (This idea is modeled after the lay therapist concept.) These paraprofessionals have the major responsibility in "mothering the mother" in an attempt to fulfill her unmet dependency needs and provide a "lifeline" which the parent can utilize in times of stress. When the mothers are ready to leave the shelter, the Social Service Assistants help them in securing better apartments; help them find jobs or job training; and teach them how to use community resources, e.g. day care centers, hospitals etc.

2. Educational activities in the program are aimed toward teaching mothers responsibilities in terms of their roles in meeting the physical and emotional needs of the child. Activities include courses on sex education, child growth and development and the child's medical needs, given by a pediatric nurse. Child Development Groups are conducted by a psychiatric social worker. Films and discussions are utilized to help the mother understand developmental stages. Consumer Education sessions, given by a member of the Home Economics Department of Hunter College, are aimed at giving the mother some experience in budgeting and shopping. The Arts and Crafts course is aimed at helping the parent with home furnishings and decoration.

3. A Therapeutic Nursery for infants: Parent stimulates child under supervision of an Early Childhood Development Expert to learn the best ways of teaching and responding to the child. A psychologist teaches parents what the child's needs are and how to best fulfill those needs. A videotape feedback confrontation technique is used to affect the behavior of the children by enlisting the mother's help as therapist. With the use of video feedback, the opportunity to record a segment of typical interaction during a play and feeding session between parent and child can

immediately be used to confront the mother with her own pattern of reacting. With such highly relevant and appropriate data available immediately after the occurrence, the learning impact is enhanced. This has proven to be an important modality in effecting behavior modification.

4. After Care. This is a very important aspect of the program. The mother with her child remains in the Shelter Residential Program for three to four months and if it is determined that she is ready to assume the care of her child in the community, she is discharged and becomes a participant of the after-care program for one year. During this year, she is visited in her home at least twice a week by her Social Service Assistant who is continuously on call for an emergency; returns to the Center for individual therapy; returns to the Center weekly for group therapy; and is visited once a week at home by a Visiting Nurse.

In summary: This model program is an innovative approach to the problem of child maltreatment combining psychiatric, medical and social services in the treatment of the parents and the child.

Objectives of Child Abuse Preventive and Treatment Programs

1. To prevent separation of parents and child whenever possible.
2. To prevent the placement of children in institutions.
3. To encourage the attainment of self-care status on the part of parents.
4. To stimulate the attainment of self-sufficiency for the family unit.
5. To prevent further abuse or neglect by removing children from families who show an unwillingness or inability to profit from the treatment program.

There are seven components to the Model Program at the Foundling Center:

1. Multidisciplinary team approach — professionals and nonprofessionals.

2. Engagement of the surrogate mothers or "lay therapists."
3. "Hot line" or "Lifeline" service for crisis situations.
4. In-resident facility for mother and child.
5. "Half-way House" — Agency Operated Boarding Home for mothers and children.
6. Outpatient "I Care" program providing family supportive services.
7. Nursery providing play therapy, crisis intervention and pediatric services.

Until recently, few efforts were made to rehabilitate abusive parents. Therapy was rarely offered to them. Unfortunately, a punitive, antiparent view is still advocated by many laymen as well as by a number of professionals. Nevertheless, it has been conclusively proven that rehabilitation is possible in the majority of cases. Where such help is given it assures both child and parent of a positive and satisfying relationship. The work done to rehabilitate abusing parents may be slow and tedious. But it is certainly effective and worthwhile.

TREATMENT OF SEXUAL ABUSE

The damaging psychological effects suffered by the sexually assaulted child are compounded frequently by the attitudes of those involved in its initial discovery and by investigative actions that follow. The questioning of the child, for example, is an emotionally charged proceeding. Also the physical examination necessary to ascertain penetration, injury or possible evidence of genital infections is frightening for the child. Together with the parents' possible verbal and psychological abuse, these questions and examinations intensify the emotional crisis.

Many cases of sexual child abuse seen in a hospital's emergency room pose a dilemma for the attending medical staff. They lack experience in handling child sexual assaults, and, all too often, there is a tendency for the examining physician to dismiss the sexually abused child as not a "real" case. In diagnosing sexual abuse or incest, it is important that there be a high index of suspicion, followed by medical care that is sympathetic and professional. The therapeutic approach must encompass sensitivity, empathy and appropriate medical intervention while, at the same time, giving due consideration to the emotions of the sexually assaulted child, the accused perpetrator and the multitroubled family unit. A sympathetic, sensitive handling of the child may elicit information that can be of importance in the diagnosis and treatment of the case.

Medical professionals attending the child must deal with parental reactions to the assault, as well as with their relationship with the child. If the incident is dealt with reasonably and calmly, with the child separated from the parents during interrogation, the child can be protected from further physical and psychological damage. If the physician is to maximize his effectiveness in dealing with all children who have been abused, sexually or otherwise, he must establish a relationship of mutual respect. A good patient-physician relationship is probably the most crucial factor in achieving a trusting rapport and the patient's compliance with treatment plans. Of course the way a physician relates to the child and the parents is influenced by his own personality and by his approach to the management of the child abuse cases.

It is the physician's responsibility to explain to the child and to the parents what to expect from the interrogation, the physical examination and the various treatment processes. Any confrontation with the parents should be simple, direct and not undertaken in anger. The discussions may involve the possible reasons for seeking medical intervention as well as reasons for the disturbing, deviant parental behavior. When confrontation is necessary, the parents should be given an opportunity to express their side of the story. The physician may find it necessary to question the child's account of the assault, or he may question the parents' account, if it does not adequately explain the child's physical or mental condition on admission to the medical facility. Signs and symptoms of emotional trauma should be observed and recorded together with the child's description of the events that took place during the sexual assault.

Physical examination of the child and the writing of a complete medical history are important steps in preparing for the treatment process. It is essential that the medical personnel attending a case of sexual child abuse be aware that all such documentation, plus the victim's medical history, become the legal documents that may serve as important evidence in possible court proceedings. For this reason, the medical record must be written accurately. Oftentimes, if there is a conflict, the hospital record is accepted in the courts over the child's own testimony. Medical personnel must be prepared to testify and to corroborate medical information during any court proceedings. Last but not least, the responsibility of the medical professionals includes continuing support to the sexually abused or molested child by providing their expert testimony in court.

Before undergoing any physical examination, the child should be told what the examination will consist of; consent forms should be signed for all procedures and treatment. During the examination itself, the child's need for privacy must be respected. The child should be partially clothed while being examined. If the child is in pain or in a disturbed mental state, the examination should be postponed and the child tranquilized or sedated.

The physician should record the child's general physical appearance and emotional state. A general physical examination should include any evidences of physical trauma such as hematomas, bruises, bite marks, lacerations, abrasions or injuries to the genital area. Physical evidences of trauma should be documented by taking colored photographs of the injury.

The pelvic examination, in the case of a girl, should be gentle and should include a careful inspection of the external genitalia, the urethra, vagina, cervix and anus. Laboratory tests for the presence of semen are necessary to substantiate incest or rape. Additional laboratory procedures, including endocervical and rectal cultures, should be undertaken to ascertain the possible existence of such venereal diseases as gonorrhea, syphilis or genital herpes. Incest should be suspected in any young child having a history of vaginitis, inflammation of the vagina, or vaginal discharge.

Since almost all state laws require physicians or other health personnel to report to child protective agencies any suspected case of sexual assault on a child, hospitals should develop a protocol for the examination and treatment of those children. Hospital emergency rooms should have administrative policy prominently displayed for the medical staff. Although progress is being made in alerting the public to issues involving such areas as legislation, investigation and prevention, there is an urgent need to improve the medical and psychological care and treatment given to the sexually abused child.

Just as in cases involving the physical abuse and neglect of children, the child that suffers sexual abuse must receive the attention of a multidisciplinary team — this includes the medical practitioner, the psychiatrist, the social worker and the court. Ideally, the therapeutic approach should be similar to that now available to the physically abused child. In addition, the adult offender and the family require ongoing treatment and rehabilitation. If the accused is not amenable to treatment, refuses treatment, is drug addicted, alcoholic or psychotic, then medical and legal intervention becomes necessary.

In situations where a family member is responsible for the sexual assault of the child, psychological intervention is usually indicated for the entire family unit. Therapy to the troubled family must be long-term, supportive and must extend beyond dealing only with the immediate crisis. It is extremely important that the medical care given to the child and to the family be sympathetic *and* professional.

LEGAL RESPONSIBILITIES

Constructive use of the laws governing society should safeguard the rights of the abused child, parent and physician. Immediate assistance must be made available to the abused child by the appropriate community and child welfare service. The utilization of law enforcement agents is to be considered if the child is a victim of severe abusive parental action leading to hospitalization or to death. Law enforcement agents should also be informed if appropriate child protective agencies are not available in the community. The results of severe abusive parental injury on a child often require the prompt removal of the patient from the threatening and hazardous home environment. In certain states, children's aid societies and The Society for the Prevention of Cruelty to Children have taken on a major role in assuming responsibilities and providing maximum protection for the maltreated child.

The juvenile and family courts are available to review petitions for prosecutions. The courts also are established to protect the parents through the acceptance of evidence which casts guilt upon the parent beyond any reasonable doubt.

The physicians are the first line of defense in the fight to decrease the incidence of the maltreatment syndrome in children. In order that this can be fully accomplished, they must be legally free to report and take positive responsible action to protect the abused child with no fear of possible personal or professional reprisal.

The Advisory Committee to the Children's Division of The American Humane Association strongly urged that state legislation be proposed making it mandatory to report cases of suspected inflicted injuries on children. The passage of such a law in all states has aided in case findings and has assured safety to the victims of childhood neglect and abuse. The Committee recommended:

1. That such legislation be directed to medical practitioners and hospital personnel coming in contact with children for the purpose of examination and treatment of injuries sustained allegedly from accidental or other causes.
2. That doctors and hospital personnel have mandatory responsibility for reporting all cases of child injury where medical diagnosis and findings are incompatible with alleged history of how injuries were sustained and the syndrome leads to the inference of "inflicted injuries."
3. That doctors and hospital staff members reporting cases of suspected inflicted injuries be made immune to possible civil or criminal action for the disclosure of matters which might be considered confidential because of the doctor-patient relationship.
4. That all reports of cases of suspected inflicted injuries be made to the public or voluntary child welfare service which carries the child protective function in the community.

Protective agencies must relate to the judicial authority in the community, and it is through these courts that plans are made to adequately care for the neglected or abused child.

In 1966, the Committee on the Infant and Preschool Child of the American Academy of Pediatrics recognized the problem of child abuse by issuing recommendations guiding legislation in this area. The Committee published the following principles:

1. Physicians should be required to report suspected cases of child abuse immediately to the agency legally charged with the responsibility of investigating child abuse, preferably the county or state department of welfare or health or their local representatives or to the nearest law enforcement agency.
2. The agency should have ample personnel and resources to take action immediately upon receipt of the report.
3. Reported cases should be investigated promptly and appropriate service provided for the child and family.
4. The child should be protected by the agency either by continued hospitalization, supervision at home or removal from home through family or juvenile court action when indicated.
5. The agency should keep a central register of all such cases. Provision should be made for the removal of case records from the register when it is found that abuse did not in fact occur.
6. The reporting physician or hospital should be granted immunity from suit.

At a meeting of the Department of Health, Education and Welfare, Children's Bureau in January 1962, measures for preventing physical abuse of infants and young children were given consideration and recommendations were proposed. Those present considered the exploration of possible mandatory reporting of cases of maltreatment in children by physicians in hospitals. It was agreed that the purpose of reporting these cases of maltreatment should result in the protection of the child rather than criminal action against the parents involved.

The first state to enact such a law was California. Under this

California law, doctors, hospital administrators and pharmacists are required to report to the law enforcement agent certain types of injuries "which have been inflicted upon a person in violation of any penal law of the State." It defines as a misdemeanor the "willful cruelty toward a child" and as a felony the "infliction of traumatic injury upon wife or child."

This law was passed several years ago but was inoperative until definite diagnostic techniques were developed which revealed injuries in various stages of resolution as seen on X-ray of the affected parts. Today there are child abuse reporting laws in all fifty states and the District of Columbia designed to require that physicians, nurses, osteopaths, teachers, dentists, social workers and other hospital administrators report cases of child abuse which are observed in the course of their professional practice. Under these state laws, the aim is to protect the child from further abuse and neglect. The reporting agent's action sets into motion the child protective agency in the community. The reporter of the child abuse is granted immunity from damage suits for false accusation. Most laws abrogate the physician-patient and husband-wife privilege as grounds for excluding evidence.

Many authorities in the field of child protection feel that a law making it mandatory to report child neglect and abuse is not an absolute necessity in the prevention of this disease. They feel that the moral obligation of all those responsible for the care of children, including physicians, hospital administrators, nurses, social service workers and pharmacists, should dictate the necessity of bringing these children to the attention of the child protective agencies. The law, however, would serve the purpose of bringing this most important disease to the attention of society and the medical-legal departments of our community. It would, perhaps, also serve to lessen the fears of physicians in reporting suspected brutality to children.

Mrs Katherine B. Oettinger, Chief of the Children's Bureau, has aptly stated:

> Even though a mandatory reporting law in a sense takes the
> physician "off the hook," since he can honestly say he has no

choice but to report, he may feel that if he reports a case he will only be opening a Pandora's box, that there are really no effective community policies existing for helping the parents with their emotional problems or for protecting the child. When the physician hesitates to report, there is something wrong in relation to follow-up social services available in his community or a breakdown in communiations.

The law would undoubtedly make it easier for the members of society and the child protective agencies to cooperate in the best interests of children when this type of problem is involved. The law would also serve as an expression of public policy in terms of concern for children.

Those interested in the legal aspects of the problem of maltreatment of children have questioned the type of legal authority granted by the law in the protection of the child. It is stressed by many that punitive aspects of such a law should be minimized, and they advocate the exclusion of the law as part of a criminal act.

Expression has been directed toward the salvation of children, hoping that with adequate service parents can be helped in keeping their families intact. It is felt that retributive or punitive action toward the parents, without thought of rehabilitation, yields little benefit for the children involved. This group also states that the penalty clause should not be part of an act primarily drafted for the protection of children and the rehabilitation of families. While there is general acceptance that neglect and abuse of children should be brought to the attention of child protective agencies and the courts, there is a divergence of opinion with respect to the type of agency in the community that should receive reports on abused children.

The selection of an agency to which a physician should report his case of child abuse or neglect should offer statewide coverage; should have authority, first, to investigate and, secondly, to initiate appropriate legal action; personnel sufficient in number and training to conduct an effective investigation; legal jurisdiction with respect to the geographical area in which the injury occurred or the child has residence; and twenty-four-hour-a-day, seven-day-a-week service on an emergency basis as the need arises.

A central registry of cases and suspects of child abuse and neglect should be maintained in the child welfare agency or social service department for the purpose of facilitating the regular follow-up on these children. This agency should also serve as a reporting area where physicians could question suspicious cases and where all pertinent information about a child victim could be expeditously gathered in time to stave off further injury and possibly death itself.

The enactment of Title V by Congress saw the creation of public welfare service and the entry of a public agency into the child protective field. The Advisory Council on Child Welfare Services, created by Congress several years ago for the purpose of making recommendations to the secretary of the Department of Health, Education and Welfare, clearly confirmed the concept that public welfare services must become available in every community to protect the child. In its report to the department, it recommended adoption of a new definition of child welfare which specifically spells out responsibility for child protective services. The significant phrase in the definition is "preventing neglect, abuse and exploitation; helping overcome problems that result in dependency, neglect or delinquency."

If the child welfare agencies are to be the reporting bureau for cases of childhood neglect and abuse, it must be clearly stated that these agencies give twenty-four-hour service on an immediate basis when such cases are reported by the physician, hospital administrator or social service worker. Again it must be mentioned that time is of the essence and every hour may mean the possible loss of life. For this reason, the agency to which the cases of child maltreatment are to be reported according to law must be provided with the necessary facilities, tools and personnel to fulfill their function. These facilities and services must be available immediately and must be ready to meet the wide range of problems included in the maltreatment syndrome of children.

All steps must first be taken to protect the child by whatever means possible but, at the same time, steps must also be taken to protect many of these parents from facing punishment and criminal prosecution. This punitive action does not correct the underlying cause of the abuse. Psychodynamics involved in the actions of these individuals must be studied and evaluated before prosecution and punishment are undertaken.

If criminal prosecution of parents is prematurely used it may prevent parents from seeking medical attention soon enough, or perhaps not at all, for fear of legal entanglement and possible criminal prosecution. In other words, it may motivate failure to get medical help until the situation becomes critical and a child's welfare may be jeopardized. There have been documented cases where parents explain that their failure to give prompt medical attention was due to fear of prosecution. These cases have apparently occurred in communities where child protective services were not available and reporting to the police was the customary procedure.

If a community agency or a child protective group cannot make the environmental changes necessary for the security of the neglected and abused child, then these agencies must appeal to the courts for their cooperative assistance. The social service workers and/or the child protective agencies, after investigations, petition the courts for assistance in removing the child from the parents. Such a court may be a special court created to handle only matters relating to children, or it may be a special part of a county, district or probate court. In some jurisdictions, it is a specialized court with broad jurisdiction covering marital or family problems as a domestic relations court, a juvenile court or a family court. Most of the juvenile courts have exclusive jurisdiction over neglected or delinquent children within age limits prescribed by law in each state.

Criminal action in cases of child abuse rarely results in conviction of the guilty parent even in those cases where it has led to death of the child. Practically all of these crimes are committed behind closed doors and "shuttered" windows making it almost impossible to prove beyond a reasonable doubt that the crime was committed by the parent. Only in cases of manslaughter when a parent confesses to the crime of child beating and death is the perpetrator of the action punished. For this reason, civil proceedings are encouraged wherein the preponderance of evidence and the concept of *res ipsa loquitur* may be applied as an effective means of protecting the abused child by removal from the parents. In civil justice, the medical evidences of child abuse (photographs of injuries, x-rays and other objective evidence) are accepted by the courts as strong testimony that the injuries sustained by the child "speak for themselves." Judge Harold A. Felix of the Family Court of the State of New York established a precedent when he rendered his opinion in a case of child abuse by stating:

> Therefore, in this type of proceeding affecting a battered child syndrome, I am borrowing from the evidentiary law of negligence the principle of *res ipsa loquitur* and accepting the proposition that the condition of the child speaks for itself, thus permitting an inference of neglect to be drawn from proof of the child's age and condition and that the latter is such as in the ordinary course of things does not happen if the parent who has the responsibility and control of an infant is protective and nonabusive.

It is a basic philosophy in all these courts that justice for children is given first consideration, followed by parental therapy as a substitution for legal punishment. The court's attitude at present considers first the child and his needs, and not the offense of any criminal action taken by the parents.

The medical and social problems involved have become more fully understood in recent years, but unfortunately, there has been a lack of keeping pace with this problem by the courts. In the past, cases of gross neglect and abuse have been brought to the courts and, in view of insufficient evidence, the child has been returned to the parents. It is certainly most difficult to prove inflicted injury by the parents, since this malicious abuse is usually done without any witnesses. The court is naturally guided by the dictum "the child belongs to the mother, and the mother belongs to the child." In a great many of these cases where the courts have decided to return the child to an offending parent, these children have again been brought to hospitals with inflicted trauma — many of them close to death.

Paulsen has emphasized that leaving a child in his home, when he bears the marks of unusual injuries which seem to have been intentionally inflicted, is taking a chance with the child's life. He further states: "Not all doubts should be resolved in favor of parents. Those who seek a court order to remove a child from a dangerous situation should not have to disprove every plausible explanation of the child's wounds. Parents have a right to their children, but their children have a right to live."

In view of our recent experiences with child abuse cases and the courts, it should be the responsibility of the courts to evaluate more closely the reports of the social service workers and the objective medical evidence presented by the physician before making a decision on the advisability of returning the child to an environment which may prove hazardous. The courts should also recognize the needs of the parents involved in this type of problem and be aware of the services that are available to them in order that they can receive the indicated guidance and counseling. In this way, they can be helped in accepting their responsibilities as parents and ultimately have their children return to the home.

If removal is considered by the courts, with social planning to be in the best interest of the child, then definitive steps are taken to have the child placed in a foster home or other child-caring institutions with available trained social service personnel. It cannot be too strongly stressed that removal of the child at this time by the court should serve two purposes: first, rehabilitation of the parents in order to properly receive the child once again; secondly, removal of the child until the home is made a better and more secure place in which to live.

Another void is experienced in the protection of the maltreated child with reference to the court and protective services, namely, that after recommendations are made by the courts to have the child removed from the immediate family, social service workers have, in many instances, encountered unfortunate stopgaps. In many parts of the country there are too few child-caring institutions with the resources necessary for the placement of children while away from home. The lack of an adequate number of foster homes makes it impossible for the court, and in many of these cases, these children must be returned to the family unit. This has often proved very detrimental to the physical and mental welfare of the child.

This entire problem of treating and preventing neglect and abuse of children depends on the cooperative efforts of all disciplines, the social, medical and legal agencies and personnel who are responsible for the care and maintenance of childhood health.

The court's recommendations cannot be carried out in areas where facilities and services for children simply do not exist. Voluntary and public agencies must be made available to provide shelter care, detention care, institutional or foster care and homemakers for these families when so ordered by the court. Only in this way can these children be adequately protected from future neglect and abuse, and the parents given the assistance and therapeutic help that can lead to better parental care.

In the process of protecting children, the court must maintain objectivity on the basis of evidence produced and judge without assuming the role of a social worker, psychiatrist or family counselor. All information from the children's social service agencies and the child protective agency in the community, in conjunction with the physician's diagnostic medical evidence, should be made available to serve the courts with the facts necessary for rendering a decision without any unnecessary time-consuming prolongation of neglect cases.

In summary: Protection and prevention of the neglect and abuse of children rests upon the concise and complete casework services by the child protective agencies exploring the complaints of abuse or neglect. Medical diagnosis is added to the evaluation of the abuse and/or neglect findings which are then presented for the action of the courts to evaluate the standards of child care in the particular family. If the child's needs are best served by the immediate removal from the family, a neglect petition is filed. Acceptance of the petition by the court begins the judicial process which leads to curtailment or nullification of parental rights in the best interests of the children.

It has been stated that no law can be better than its implementation, and its implementation can be no better than the resources permit. Preventive and therapeutic psychiatric community services for the parents must be made available. Child-caring institutions, trained social workers, foster homes, homemakers and day care centers are necessary if the plight of the maltreated child is to be improved.

8

THE LEGAL FRAMEWORK FOR CHILD PROTECTION*

FOR too long, child maltreatment has been a hidden problem, relegated to understaffed and overwhelmed protective agencies far from public view. Only in recent years has the true seriousness of child abuse and child neglect been widely recognized.

In the 1960s, the plight of the "battered child" was brought to public attention, largely through the efforts of leaders in the medical profession. Legislative action quickly followed. In 1963, the United States Children's Bureau published a guide for child abuse legislation, based on the new concept of reporting child abuse to a state central register of records. In the context of the times, the 1963 Model Child Protection Act was an innovative document. Within three years, every state enacted a reporting law, many patterned after the Children's Bureau model.

By the 1970s, widespread concern over endangered children had broadened to include all elements of the "Maltreatment Syndrome" so that over forty states had amended their laws to require the reporting of suspected child neglect as well as child abuse. Reporting laws were also expanded to include important ancillary provisions for immunity for good faith reporting, penalities for failure to report, protective custody and the abrogation of certain privileged communications. Over thirty states have laws which establish a central register of reports, and an increasing number of states are legislatively prescribing procedures for case handling and case management.

The Federal Child Abuse Prevention and Treatment Act re-

*The opinions expressed herein do not necessarily reflect the position or policy of the Department of Health, Education and Welfare, and no official endorsement by the Department should be inferred.

flects this evolution toward improved and expanded child protective laws. Its eligibility criteria for state grants describe the essential fundamentals of an effective statewide child protection system. Section 4 (b) (2) of the Act provides:

> (2) In order for a State to qualify for assistance under this subsection, such State shall:
>
> (A) have in effect a State child abuse and neglect law which shall include provisions for immunity for persons reporting instances of child abuse and neglect from prosecution, under any State or local law, arising out of such reporting;
>
> (B) provide for the reporting of known and suspected instances of child abuse and neglect;
>
> (C) provide that upon receipt of a report of known or suspected instances of child abuse or neglect an investigation shall be initiated promptly to substantiate the accuracy of the report, and, upon a finding of abuse or neglect, immediate steps shall be taken to protect the health and welfare of the abused or neglected child, as well as that of any other child under the same care who may be in danger of abuse or neglect;
>
> (D) demonstrate that there are in effect throughout the State, in connection with the enforcement of child abuse and neglect laws and with the reporting of suspected instances of child abuse and neglect, such administrative procedures, such personnel trained in child abuse and neglect prevention and treatment, such training procedures, such institutional and other facilities (public and private), and such related multidisciplinary programs and services as may be necessary or appropriate to assure that the State will deal effectively with child abuse and neglect cases in the State;
>
> (E) provide for methods to preserve the confidentiality of all records in order to protect the rights of the child, his parents or guardians;
>
> (F) provide for the cooperation of law enforcement officials, courts of competent jurisdiction, and appropriate State agencies providing human services;
>
> (G) provide that in every case involving an abused or neglected child which results in a judicial proceeding a

guardian *ad litem* shall be appointed to represent the child in such proceeding;

(H) provide that the aggregate of support for programs or projects related to child abuse and neglect assisted by State funds shall not be reduced below the level provided during fiscal year 1973, and set forth policies and procedures designed to assure that Federal funds made available under this Act for any fiscal year will be so used as to supplement and, to the extent practicable, increase the level of State funds which would, in the absence of Federal funds, be available for such programs and projects;

(I) provide for dissemination of information to the general public with respect to the problem of child abuse and neglect and the facilities and prevention and treatment methods available to combat instances of child abuse and neglect; and

(J) to the extent feasible, insure that parental organizations combating child abuse and neglect receive preferential treatment.

Although these requirements merely state the indispensable fundamentals of an effective child protective system, a number of states have had difficulty implementing them because they often require substantial legislative and programmatic upgrading. The provisions of the Model Child Protection Act reflect and conform to the requirements for state eligibility specified in the Federal Child Abuse Prevention and Treatment Act. Although a state may be deemed eligible for a state grant without enacting the provisions of the Model Act, the Model Act has been designed so that any state adopting it would automatically satisfy the state law requirements of the federal law. (However, the Model Act cannot deal with those issues of eligibility involving programmatic and procedural requirements.)

Although the Model Act is intended to assist states seeking to meet federal eligibility requirements, its provisions go beyond the minimum requirements in the federal law. The Model Act is being offered as a living instrument to assist *all* states seeking to improve the necessary legal framework for an effective and fair child protection system.

PHILOSOPHY OF THE MODEL ACT

Abused and neglected children are in urgent need of protection. But there are no provisions in the Model Act for punishment, because in most situations criminal intent is not present. The purposes of the Act are curative and remedial.

Child maltreatment is primarily caused by social and psychological ills. The best way to protect a child is to deal with these underlying ills. Often, a family's ability to care for and protect its children can be strengthened by appropriate treatment and ameliorative services.

Unfortunately, though, families frequently do not seek help on their own. Hence, the Model Act attempts to assist and encourage parents to seek help in meeting their child care responsibilities. But if parents do not act on their own, some third person must take protective action. In the past, though, many private citizens and professionals have failed to report substantial numbers of children whose condition indicated that they were abused or neglected. Therefore, the Model Act seeks to encourage fuller reporting by establishing simplified reporting procedures and by establishing a fair and effective state and local child protection system that can handle the increased reports that will result. In each county a child protective service is established to swiftly and competently investigate reports of known or suspected child abuse and neglect, while maintaining due process and fundamental fairness to parents.

The most important aspect of the Model Act is its emphasis on the development of services to go along with increased reporting. It would have been far easier — there would have been less work and less controversy — if only a reporting law were proposed. But to do so would be to ignore the increased reports that inevitably flow from an improved reporting law. Unless a system for handling the increased reports is established, strengthening reporting requirements and improving reporting techniques can work to the detriment of agency and family welfare.

Whenever a family needs services, the Model Act requires that they be offered first on a voluntary basis. The protective agency is to resort to court only if necessary. [See sections 16(g), (h), (j) and (k).] When the powers of a court must be invoked to protect a child, the Model Act favors resort to a civil proceeding in a family or juvenile court. Though referral to a criminal court may be appropriate in certain situations, the criminal court can protect a child only by jailing an offending parent. The juvenile court, on the other hand, can help provide social and psychological services necessary to deal with some of the fundamental problems which lead to abuse and neglect.

Ultimately, however, efforts to preserve and improve family stability are, and must remain, the province of community resources and agencies with a broader and more long-range responsibility towards children and families than that of a public, child protective service agency. The Model Act does not seek to shift this fundamental social welfare responsibility away from community resources and agencies already involved successfully in helping children and families nor does it seek to discourage the development of additional community-based treatment and prevention programs. Indeed, through its provisions for a community child protection advisory board, interdisciplinary teams, a local plan for child protective services and the authorization for the child protective service to purchase the services of other agencies, the Model Act seeks to encourage existing agencies to assume greater treatment responsibility and to expand their treatment capacity.

Finally, the Model Act recognizes that institutional child abuse and neglect is more widespread than we would like to believe. Therefore, the Act makes provision for the appropriate handling of reports of the abuse and neglect of children who live in public and private *residential* facilities.

Emphasis on Self-Help and
Voluntarily Sought Services

In the United States, there has been a traditional and fundamental reliance on self-help for personal problems and on voluntarily sought social and child welfare services. Key to the effectiveness of any child protection system is its ability to offer services on a voluntary basis. From practical and humanitarian points of view, it is preferable that families needing help seek it on their own. Experience has shown that services are more effective when sought or accepted voluntarily — many parents will seek out help, or will accept it when it is offered, if they understand their need for it. Parents must be assisted and encouraged to find the help they need.

The Model Act reaffirms this traditional and fundamental reliance on voluntarily sought social and child welfare services by encouraging parents to seek help through the procedures and agencies established by the Act and through other means as well. Examples of such assistance include traditional family counseling and mental health services, and such newer, specialized resources for families in trouble as the following ones: Parents Anonymous; hot lines, helplines, and other telephone counseling services; child development, parent effectiveness, and infant stimulation centers; and crisis nurseries and drop-in services. Thus, for example, Section 3 is careful to ensure that parents calling on the statewide hot line who need assistance will be directed to those services that seem most appropriate for them.

Unified Definition of
"Child Abuse and Neglect"

The increased formality and legal strictures surrounding contemporary child protection work require that the terms "child abuse" and "child neglect" be clearly and carefully defined to meet the objectives they are meant to serve. The definitions of "child abuse" and "child neglect" used in the Model Act unify all forms of child maltreatment, including child battering, physical attack, dependency, abandonment, and failure to provide food, clothing, shelter, and other necessities, in one conceptual framework — the "abused or neglected child."

Artificially created distinctions between "child abuse" and "child neglect" have often caused harmful differences in the handling of cases. But, as made clear by the concept of the "maltreatment syndrome," the harm done to a child because of inadequate parental care can be just as severe and long lasting as the harm caused by physical battering. Indeed, child abuse and child neglect often occur together and are interrelated problems falling, in large part, within the concept of the "maltreated child." (See section 4.)

Even before passage of the Federal Child Abuse Prevention and Treatment Act of 1974, which requires states to provide for the reporting of child neglect as well as abuse in order to receive special grants, all states were broadening the circumstances requiring a report. Increasing numbers of states have concluded that physical abuse, child battering, sexual abuse, child neglect, abandonment, emotional abuse and emotional neglect are all aspects of the same problem — the inadequate parental care of children. They realize that to single out one form of maltreatment for special attention is to establish false and dangerously misleading distinctions. Child neglect can be as damaging and just as deadly as child abuse.

As a result, most states have experienced phenomenal increases in the number of reports of known and suspected child abuse and child neglect. But it is important to note that broadening the circumstances that must be reported does not necessarily increase the actual number of cases brought to the attention of the authorities. It may mean only that cases which were once handled outside the mandated reporting process — by police, welfare agencies, child protective agencies, and courts — are now handled within it.

Reporting of Known and Suspected Child Abuse and Neglect

When parents faced with child abuse and child neglect problems do not seek help on their own, the responsibility to take protective action rests with others. But before social service and other helping agencies can assist children and parents, they must learn of the child's predicament. Someone — a friend, a neighbor, a relative, or a concerned professional — must recognize the child's danger and report it. If a case of suspected child abuse or child neglect is not reported, a protective agency cannot become involved, emergency protective measures cannot be taken, and a treatment plan cannot be developed.

Although the early recognition and reporting of suspected child abuse and neglect are the first essential steps in preventing further maltreatment, many physicians, nurses, social workers, teachers and others do not report the abuse or neglect that they see. The reluctance of many professionals to take action to protect children resulted in the development and passage of laws in all states which require, under penalty, certain professionals to report known and suspected child abuse and neglect.

The medical professional was the first, and remains the foremost, target of reporting statutes. But the early focus on physicians (who were considered the professionals most likely to see injured children) quickly expanded to include all professionals in the healing arts, and has since broadened to include teachers, social workers, police, clergymen and coroners, among others. In addition, an increasing number of states (over twenty at this writing) require "any person" to report known and suspected child abuse and neglect.

The Model Act continues this approach by requiring certain professionals to report, because of their frequent contact with children and because their training and experience should make them sensitive to possible abuse and neglect in the children they see. [See section 5.] In addition, anyone is permitted to report when they have reasonable cause to suspect that a child is abused or neglected. [See section 6.]

State reporting laws are most notable for what they do *not* require. They do not require that the individual making the report be certain a child is abused or neglected. They require only that the individual "suspect," "reasonably suspect," "have reason to believe," or "have cause to believe" that a child is abused or neglected. Under the Model Act, specified professionals must report if they have *"reasonable cause to suspect"* that a child is abused or neglected. This statutory language is intended to ensure the fullest possible reporting.

"Reasonable cause to suspect" can include the nature of the child's injuries, the history of prior injuries to a child, the condition of a child, his personal hygiene and his clothing, the statements and demeanor of a child or parent (especially if the injuries to the child are at variance to the parental explanation of them), the condition of the home and the statements of others.

Because in the past cumbersome and confusing reporting procedures have discouraged more complete reporting, the Model Act is careful to establish simple and easy to use reporting procedures. [See section 13.]

After a report is made, the child protective agency is responsible for determining the child's true condition and for beginning the process of diagnosis, protection, and treatment.

Protective Custody

In most child abuse and neglect situations, the child does not have to be removed from his parents' custody in order to protect his well-being and future development. Indeed, in many situations, removal may be harmful to the child. The child may see separation from his parents as a deprivation or as a punishment for the child's inadequacy. Removal may be counterproductive to any treatment effort; it may destroy the fragile family fabric and make it more difficult for the parents to cope with the child when he is returned to their care. Moreover, the conditions of substitute care are also often unsuitable for the child's optimum care and development.

However, sometimes a child has to be removed from his home against parental wishes for his own safety. Often such removal must occur before court action is possible, because the child may be further harmed during the time necessary to obtain a court order. In most states, the police are already authorized to take children into protective custody, either through specific child protective legislation or their general law enforcement powers. The right of physicians and social workers to place children in protective custody is gaining wider acceptance. The Model Act continues such procedures. [See section 9.]

Nevertheless, there is always the danger of careless or automatic — though well-meaning — exercise of the power to place a child in protective custody. In too many situations, past practice has been to remove a child from his home first — and to ask questions later. The Model Act seeks to prevent the indiscriminate use of protective custody by imposing two conditions for such emergency protective custody: (1) The child must be in imminent danger, and (2) there must be no time to apply for a court order. Only in such grave and urgent situations may a child be removed without prior court approval. Examples of such situations include the following: when children are being attacked or are in imminent danger of being attacked by their parents; when children need immediate food, clothing, shelter, or medical care; when young children are left alone unattended; or when it appears that the entire family may disappear before the facts can be sorted out. [See section 9(a).]

Because the correctness of the protective custody decision should be reviewed by a court as soon as possible, the Model Act establishes a twenty-four-hour time limit for holding a child without a court order. By that time, there is no reason why a judge cannot be reached. The possibility of disturbing a judge on a weekend is a small price to pay for ensuring that the initial decision is reviewed promptly. [See sections 9(d) and (e).]

Immunity from Liability

Immunity from liability for reporting in good faith is essential to any child protective system which must rely on third party reporting. Otherwise, fears of unjust lawsuits for libel, slander, defamation, invasion of privacy or breach of confidentiality may discourage reporting. Even though good faith on the part of the reporter would probably be a defense against such lawsuits, all states specifically grant mandated reporters immunity from civil liability for good faith reports in order to eradicate all vestiges of uncertainty; all but one also grant immunity from criminal liability. Like a growing number of states, and in accordance with the Federal Child Abuse Prevention and Treatment Act, [Section 4(b) (2) (A)], the Model Act extends this specific grant of immunity to *any person* acting in good faith, whether or not mandated by law to report. Immunity exists only when someone is acting in "good faith." Anyone who makes a malicious report would lose this grant of immunity. [See section 10.]

Because fear of lawsuits is frequently cited as a deterrent to more complete reporting, this immunity provision should be clearly explained in any public and professional education campaign about the law. [See section 26.]

Abrogation of Privileged Communications

Child abuse and child neglect usually occur behind closed doors without witnesses. In establishing that a child has been abused and neglected, great reliance is necessarily placed on medical evidence and on the statements of the child and parents. Conversations between parents and many of the professionals most likely to learn about child abuse, such as those between doctor and patient or social worker and client, are statutorily made "privileged communications." Ordinarily, anyone subject to such a privilege is prohibited by law from divulging anything told to them by the protected person, unless permission is given. While a legal mandate to report known and suspected child abuse and neglect automatically overrides any other law about privileged communication, there are many situations where concern over the privileged nature of a communication could become an obstacle to reporting. For example, a physician might think that he could not make a report about suspicious injuries without first securing the permission of the parents.

Therefore, for purposes of reporting, cooperating with the child protective services, and testifying in court about known or suspected child abuse or neglect, the Model Act abrogates the husband-wife privilege and all professional privileges except the attorney-client privilege. Although this abrogation is absolute, protective workers, judges and prosecutors should use it with discretion, especially in situations involving spouses and treatment professionals who may have a trustful relationship with the parents. [See section 11.]

Penalties for Failure to Report

Although the ultimate success of a child protective reporting system must depend upon the professionals and private citizens who willingly cooperate with the child protective service, reporting requirements need enforceable provisions for the few who refuse to accept their legal and moral obligations to protect endangered children. Thus, the reporting laws of over half the states contain specific criminal and civil penalty clauses for failure to report. The Model Act also has one, although it limits penalties to situations in which there has been a "knowing and willful failure" to fulfill the legal obligation to report. Only professionals mandated to make reports are subject to this penalty for failure to report. [See section 12.]

Besides acting to encourage fuller reporting, penalty clauses tend to assist mandated reporters in working with parents, they make it easier for doctors, teachers, social workers, day care workers and others to explain to parents why they are making a report. In addition, experience shows that a penalty clause is invaluable to staff members of agencies and institutions who must often persuade their superiors of the necessity of making a report. (For example, nurses frequently complain that only mention of the penalty clause convinces hospital administrators to commence protective action.)

Although penalty provisions are a valuable and necessary component of an effective reporting law, it must be emphasized that the main reason for underreporting remains ignorance and misunderstanding of the reporting law and of child protective procedures. The most effective way to encourage full and accurate reporting is through professional and public education about the nature of child abuse and neglect. Private citizens but especially professionals, including child care professionals, physicians, nurses, social workers, and teachers must be made sensitive to the occurrence of child abuse and neglect, must be able to identify it, and must know how to report it. [See section 26.]

Photographs and X-rays

X-rays can be crucial to early and accurate diagnosis of child abuse and neglect. They can also play a crucial role in preserving evidence. Long after memories have faded, photographs and X-rays can provide extra assurance that subsequent child protective decision-making, and possible court action, reflect the severity of the child's initial condition, particularly when case records lack sufficient detail. A photograph or an X-ray can be worth, as the cliché goes, a thousand words. Therefore, the Model Act authorizes persons and officials required to report to take, or arrange to have taken, photographs and X-rays without parental permission, which would ordinarily be required in many circumstances. [See section 8.]

Statewide Twenty-four-hour-a-day Reporting Hot Line

In the past, the difficulty of making reports was one of the major stumbling blocks to more complete reporting. To facilitate the reporting process, the Model Act creates a twenty-four-hour-a-day, seven-day-a-week, toll-free telephone number to accept reports of known and suspected child abuse and neglect. The single statewide number is meant to encourage reporting by simplifying the reporting process and by making it easily available. It creates one easily publicized phone number for an entire state. Since the number is statewide, some people using it would have to pay for a long distance call; having a toll-free number avoids this obstacle to reporting. The number should be available twenty-four-hours-a-day because emergencies arise at all hours. States that already have such a system report there is sufficient use of the telephone number throughout the day and night to justify this procedure. [See section 13.]

Specialized Local Child Protective Agency

Strengthening reporting requirements can be detrimental to the functioning of agencies and the welfare of families unless a system is established to respond to the reports. The Model Act creates a child protective system capable of investigating reports of known or suspected child abuse and neglect swiftly and competently while maintaining due process and fundamental fairness to parents. [See sections 14, 15 and 16.]

Until recently, insufficient attention has been paid to establishing strong, viable local child protective agencies. Responsibility for the prompt and effective handling of reports of known and suspected child abuse or neglect has been dispersed among a number of public agencies which have many other, often conflicting, duties which compete for scarce resources and attention.

Because most acts of abuse or neglect happen in the privacy of the home without any witnesses, gathering information on what happened can be exceedingly difficult. If the parents are looking for help, they may tell the worker what happened, but often they deny everything the worker has learned from others. Protective caseworkers have great difficulty in getting genuine information about families, and often they are unsure of their role and responsibilities in protecting children. Many agencies are plagued with staff turnovers as high as 100 percent every year or so. The staggering responsibilities placed on protective caseworkers, and the unique skills demanded by protective work, require that protective agencies be specialized and have a highly qualified staff.

The Model Act establishes a child protective service agency in each county or comparable political subdivision of a state. The local child protective agency is the heart of the child protective system established by the Model Act. Through the local agency, the Act seeks to focus and strengthen local efforts to improve the prevention and treatment of child abuse and neglect. The existence of a single agency to receive and investigate *all* reports in each community is expected to eliminate the confusion and lack of accountability that can occur when reports are handled by a number of different agencies. In addition, the Model Act looks to the local agency, with the assistance of the Community Child Abuse and Neglect Advisory Board, described in Section 17, to identify gaps in service and to move to fill them. [See section 15.]

It is important to emphasize that no new agency need be established if an existing agency, or part of one, can provide the child protective services required by the Model Act. In states with either state administered or supervised social service departments, for example, the state department could establish or designate specialized staff units at the county or regional level; or it could choose to designate and purchase the services of another public or private agency, perhaps even sponsoring the creation of an entirely new agency. (The Model Act discourages the designation of police or law enforcement agencies because criminal intent is largely absent in abuse and neglect cases. If a community decides to empower a law enforcement agency to perform the child protective investigation, this agency should establish a specialized unit staffed by nonuniformed officers qualified to deal with the social and family problems which lie at the root of child abuse and neglect, and it should be able to make the type of referrals crucial for the successful handling of cases. Ordinarily, this would be the police youth bureau or domestic relations bureau.) [See section 14.]

The local child protective service is required to receive reports at all hours of the day or night. Investigations must commence within twenty-four hours. Thus, for example, the investigation of a report received on a Friday night must begin no later than Saturday night at the same hour. The child protective service must be able to receive and evaluate reports at all times, and it must be able to provide emergency services immediately when needed. Thus the person in the agency who receives the report must be able to assess the need for immediate action. An answering service cannot provide this kind of assessment. [See section 16.]

The purpose of the child protective investigation is to protect and enhance the health and welfare of the children and families involved by beginning the process of helping the parents to meet their child care responsibilities, instead of punishing them. Specifically, the child protective services is assigned the crucial first steps of:

(1) providing immediate protection to children, through temporary stabilization of the home environment as well as protective custody;

(2) assessing the needs of children and families;

(3) providing or arranging for protection, treatment, and ameliorative services; and,

(4) when necessary, instituting civil court action (ordinarily juvenile court action) to remove a child from a dangerous environment or to impose treatment on his family.

Even though persons not required to report (including friends, neighbors and relatives) make the largest proportion of child protective reports, regardless of the danger of the child, their reports are often given second class status; they are not recorded in the central register and are not accorded investigative priority. Distinctions based on who makes a report have no place in child protective efforts; merely because a report is made by a private citizen or nonmandated professional does not make it any less serious than one made by a legally mandated reporter. Reports from every source must be handled the same way. Of course, the child protective service should establish necessary investigative priorities based upon the actual urgency of the case — but not on the basis of who made the report. [See sections 6 and 16(a).]

After receiving a report of suspected child abuse or neglect, the protective agency makes an investigation to determine whether the child is in danger and what services should be offered the family. Protective caseworkers may contact schools, neighbors, relatives and the source of the report to obtain as complete a picture of the situation as possible. On the basis of these findings as well as interviews with the family, caseworkers evaluate the family and decide what, if anything, must be done to protect the child.

Interdisciplinary Team

Although the Model Act recommends that the child protective agency be a social service agency, no single agency can successfully perform all the important functions assigned to the child protective agency. Optimal diagnostic and treatment efforts require the contributions of a wide range of professionals and community agencies. In many parts of the country, the creation of interdisciplinary teams has succeeded in bringing the collective expertise of relevant professionals to bear in identification and treatment. Thus the Model Act requires the child protective agency to convene "one or more interdisciplinary 'Child Protective Teams' to assist it in its diagnostic, assessment, service, and coordination responsibilities." [See section 16(e).]

Community Child Protection Advisory Board

Decisive to the success of any child protective agency is its ability to engage existing community services in its efforts to create indigenous, responsive prevention and treatment programs. Ultimately, efforts to preserve and improve family stability are, and must remain, the province of community resources and agencies with a broader and more long-range responsibility toward children and families than the child protective service agency. Thus the Model Act creates the Community Child Protection Advisory Board to ensure cooperative planning and evaluation of services for endangered children and their families. [See section 17.]

The Advisory Board has major responsibilities in the formulation of the local plan for child protective services. The plan is expected to be the blueprint to establish a framework of cooperative community structures for services to prevent and treat child abuse and neglect. A key aspect of the plan is the requirement for the broadest possible public and professional consultation *during* its preparation. Part of this consultation is achieved through a public hearing held by the Advisory Board. The local plan should cover all local activities undertaken to fulfill each provision of the state's child abuse and neglect laws. [See section 18.] It is expected that the local plan will include provision on: the receipt, investigation and verification of reports; the determination of protection, treatment and ameliorative service needs; the provision of such services; when necessary, resort to criminal or juvenile court; and monitoring, evaluation and planning. The local plan should also include full descriptions of staff qualifications, training procedures, institutional or other facilities (public and private), related multidisciplinary programs and services as may be necessary, purchase of service procedures, public and professional education and training programs, cooperative interagency activities, as well as any other relevant efforts.

The provision authorizing the purchase and use of the services of other public or private agencies, it is hoped, will provide the financial backbone of the plan.

State Responsibilities

Until recently, sustained efforts at the state level to improve child abuse and neglect services have been all but impossible. Often, only one professional, sometimes titled the "child protection consultant," was assigned to child protective concerns at the state level. Sometimes, this assignment was only one of many given to a single, overburdened individual. Long-range, rational planning cannot be performed in such situations; even responding to day-to-day operational concerns becomes an unmanageable burden. Furthermore, local agencies are forced to fend for themselves, learning from trial and error, instead of benefiting from the informed guidance of state officials. Therefore, the Model Act assigns the state department with social service capabilities a broad mandate to strengthen and improve child abuse and neglect prevention and treatment efforts.

To give the state department real ability to shape the activities of local child protective agencies, the Model Act authorizes the state department to withhold state reimbursement for all or part of the local agency's activities if its annual plan for services is ultimately disapproved. Of course, this power cannot be exercised lightly. Nor is it an absolute power; the state department's decisions under this section are made reviewable through the state's Civil Procedure Law. [See section 18(f).]

State Child Abuse and Neglect Coordinating Committee

The Model Act also establishes a "State Child Abuse and

Neglect Coordinating Committee" to enhance the state department's efforts, while at the same time ensuring consultation, coordination and cooperation between the state department and other relevant state agencies. [See section 20.]

State Citizens' Committee

The Model Act establishes a "statewide Citizen's Committee on Child Abuse and Neglect" to advise the governor, the state department and the State Child Abuse and Neglect Coordinating Committee. The Citizen's Committee, made up of persons of distinction and with overlapping terms, should have an independent voice to speak out on the problems confronting the state's child protection system. [See section 22.]

Central Register of Child Protection Cases

Over forty states have established a central register of child protection cases. If designed and operated correctly, a central register can help child protective workers assess the danger to a child they suspect is being abused or neglected. By facilitating the searching and location of previous reports on the same child or his siblings, the central register can be invaluable in determining whether there is a repeating or continuing pattern of parental maltreatment. The repetition of suspicious injuries is strongly indicative of child abuse, and only through a central register or some other kind of central indexing of information can such information be gathered and reviewed. Because families in such cases often go from hospital to hospital or social service agency to social service agency, the only way a physician or protective worker can quickly know whether a prior report has been made is through a central register of reports.

Perhaps equally as important, a central register can help ensure that investigations are properly performed and services provided. If it can receive and process reports immediately and can review them for their timeliness, it can monitor the provision of services on an ongoing and continuing basis. The central register can also be used as a research tool to determine the incidence of abuse and neglect in a state and the most effective types of treatment. [See section 21.]

Confidentiality and the Right to Privacy of Those Reported

Many of the reports kept by the child protective service or stored and made easily accessible by the central register, prove to be unfounded. Sometimes they are made by malicious neighbors or relatives; more often reporters, though well intentioned, are mistaken in their suspicions. Under the Model Act, no data on a family can be kept in the register if the report turns out to be "unfounded"; all unfounded reports are removed from the register. Even when the reports in the register are true, as the majority of them are, there is still a need to protect the rights and sensibilities of those who are named in them, for these records contain information about the most private aspects of personal and family life. Improper disclosure could stigmatize the future of all those mentioned in the report. Therefore, access to data in the register is carefully limited to those professionals and officials who are responsible for making emergency decisions to protect endangered children. The data in the register is made confidential; unlawful use of it is a crime. [See sections 21(f) and 24.]

As a matter of fundamental fairness, people ought to know what information a government agency is keeping about them. The Model Act guarantees the subject of a report the right to see all the information about him in the report or register at any time. Nevertheless, the subject of the report's right to access is not absolute. The identity of any person who made the report or who cooperated with the subsequent investigation may be withheld when giving such information "likely to be detrimental to the safety or interests of such person."

Furthermore, the subject or a report may use his or her knowledge of what is in the report or request the state department to amend, expunge or remove the record from the register. If the state department does not do so, the subject has a right to a "fair hearing" similar to those held to determine whether a recipient's public assistance can be terminated. [See section 21(i).]

Institutional Child Abuse and Neglect

Unfortunately, children are sometimes abused and neglected by the very institutions meant to protect them from harm. The Model Act seeks to deal with those situations in which children are abused while living in public and private *residential* facilities. It provides for an independent investigation of all reports of institutional abuse and neglect; no agency would be allowed to investigate itself when a report of institutional abuse and neglect has been made. An outside, disinterested agency must perform this investigation. [See section 23.]

Right to Counsel in Child Protective Proceedings

Child abuse and child neglect proceedings in court have profoundly important consequences for the children and parents involved. Children can be removed from their parents and placed in foster care or institutions for months or years, even until they reach their majority. Moreover, the involuntary intrusion into the family by the court and related social agencies can be unpleasant to all involved. Therefore, the Model Act seeks to protect the right of parents and children to a full and fair judicial review before intrusion into family life is authorized by a court. Both the parents and the children must be provided with legal counsel to represent them and their wishes before the court. [See section 25.]

In addition, the Model Act recognizes that the local child protective service also needs legal assistance in the presentation of information to the court. Therefore, the Model Act also ensures that a child protective agency is also represented by counsel. [See section 25(c).]

Professional and Public Education

The key to real progress in the prevention, identification and treatment of child abuse and neglect is the support of an informed and aware citizenry coupled with the capable efforts of concerned professionals. Therefore, the last major section of the

Model Act requires a comprehensive and continuing state *and* local program of education and training for the general public and professionals, including child protective workers. [See section 26.]

Education programs should include general information on child abuse and neglect, as well as specific information on the law, reporting procedures and the child protective system. An effort should also be made to reach parents who may need help — to let them know they are not alone and where they can get help.

IMPLEMENTING THE MODEL ACT

No law is the ultimate answer to any problem. A law may prohibit child abuse and neglect, but it cannot prevent or cure it. A law may mandate the rehabilitation of parents, but it cannot rehabilitate them. A law can establish the institutional framework for the protection of children, and it can enunciate the philosophy that will motivate and guide a system as it deals with the individual problems of children and families. Ultimately, though, the prevention and treatment of child abuse and child neglect depend less on laws and more on the existence of sufficient and suitable helping services for children and parents. The law embodied in the Model Act is an essential first step in the development of a community network of prevention and treatment services. As a totality, this system may look like an impossible ideal, but each of its elements has been tried and found effective somewhere in the United States. Based on the research and experience of professionals in the field, the Model Act has provisions for the basic elements of an effective, modern child protective system.

A law lives in the way it is used. Without the dedicated support of those who must implement it, even the most far-reaching, well-intentioned law is useless. Any state considering adoption of the Model Act, in whole or part, should do so only after the broadest possible consultation with child protective professionals and the public. Those affected by the law have to be involved in its development if they are going to accept the law and work to fulfill its provisions.

9

MODEL CHILD PROTECTION ACT

SECTION 1. TITLE

This Act shall be known as the Child Protective Services Act of 1975.

SECTION 2. FINDINGS AND PURPOSE

Abused and neglected children in this state urgently need protection. It is the purpose of this Act to help save them from further injury and harm. This Act seeks to establish a fair and effective state and local child protection system by providing those procedures and services necessary to safeguard the well-being and development of endangered children and to preserve and stabilize family life, whenever appropriate. Recognizing that children also can be abused and neglected while living in public and private residential agencies and institutions meant to serve them, this Act also provides for the appropriate handling of reports of institutional child abuse and neglect.

SECTION 3. PERSONS OR FAMILIES NEEDING ASSISTANCE ENCOURAGED TO SEEK IT

Any person or family seeking assistance in meeting child care responsibilities may use, and is encouraged to use, the services and facilities established by this Act, including the single state-wide telephone number and the local child protective service. Whether or not the problem presented constitutes child abuse or neglect as defined by this Act, such persons or families shall be referred to appropriate community resources or agencies. No person seeking assistance under this section shall be required to give his name or any other identifying information.

SECTION 4. DEFINITIONS

When used in this Act and unless the specific context indicates otherwise:

(a) "Child" means a person under the age of 18.

(b) An "abused or neglected child" means a child whose physical or mental health or welfare is harmed or threatened with harm by the acts or omissions of his parent or other person responsible for his welfare.

(c) "Harm" to a child's health or welfare can occur when the parent or other person responsible for his welfare:

    (i) Inflicts, or allows to be inflicted, upon the child, physical or mental injury, including injuries sustained as a result of excessive corporal punishment; or

    (ii) Commits, or allows to be committed, against the child, a sexual offense, as defined by state law; or

    (iii) Fails to supply the child with adequate food, clothing, shelter, education (as defined by state law), or health care, though financially able to do so or offered financial or other reasonable means to do so; for the purposes of this Act, "adequate health care" includes any medical or non-medical remedial health care permitted or authorized under state law; or

    (iv) Abandons the child, as defined by state law; or

    (v) Fails to provide the child with adequate care, supervision, or guardianship by specific acts or omissions of a similarly serious nature requiring the intervention of the child protective service or a court.

(d) "Threatened harm" means a substantial risk of harm.

(e) "A person responsible for a child's welfare" includes the child's parent; guardian; foster parent; an employee of a public or private residential home, institution or agency; or other person legally responsible for the child's welfare in a residential setting.

(f) "Physical injury" means death, or permanent or temporary disfigurement or impairment of any bodily organ.

(g) "Mental injury" means an injury to the intellectual or psychological capacity of a child as evidenced by an observable and substantial impairment in his ability to function within his normal range of performance and behavior, with due regard to his culture.

(h) "Institutional child abuse and neglect" means situations of known or suspected child abuse or neglect where the person responsible for the child's welfare is a foster parent or the employee of a public or private residential home, institution, or agency.

(i) "State department" means the department designated under section 19 to have prime responsibility for state efforts to strengthen and improve the prevention, identification and treatment of child abuse and neglect.

(j) "Subject of the report" means any person reported under this Act, including any child or parent, guardian, or other person responsible for the child's welfare.

(k) "Unfounded report" means a report made pursuant to this Act for which there is no probable cause to believe that the child is abused or neglected. For the purposes of this Act, it is presumed that all reports are unfounded unless the child protective service determines otherwise.

(l) "Probable cause" means facts and circumstances based upon accurate and reliable information (including hearsay) that would justify a reasonable person to believe that a child subject to a report under this Act is abused or neglected. Such facts and circumstances may include evidence of an injury or injuries, if not satisfactorily explained, and the statements of a person worthy of belief, even if there is no present evidence of injury.

Title II: Reporting Procedure and Initial Child Protective Actions

SECTION 5. PERSONS AND OFFICIALS REQUIRED TO REPORT KNOWN AND SUSPECTED CHILD ABUSE OR NEGLECT

(a) When the following professionals and officials know or have reasonable cause to suspect that a child known to them in their professional or official capacity is an abused or neglected child, they are required to report or cause a report to be made in accordance with this Act: any physician; resident; intern; hospital personnel engaged in the admission, examination, care or treatment of persons; nurse; osteopath; chiropractor; podiatrist; medical examiner or coroner; dentist; optometrist; or any other health or mental health professional; Christian Science practitioner; religious healer; school teacher or other school official or pupil personnel; social worker, professional day care center or any other professional child care, foster care, residential, or institutional worker; or peace officer or other law enforcement official.

(b) Whenever a person is required to report under this Act in his capacity as a member of the staff of a medical or other public or private institution, school, facility, or agency, he shall immediately notify the person in charge, or his designated agent, who shall then become responsible to make the report or cause the report to be made. However, nothing in this section or Act is intended to relieve individuals of their obligation to report on their own behalf, unless a report already has been made or will be made forthwith.

SECTION 6. ANY PERSON PERMITTED TO REPORT

Any person may make a report under this Act, if he knows or has reasonable cause to suspect that a child is abused or neglected.

SECTION 7. MANDATORY REPORTING OF DEATHS TO AND POSTMORTEM INVESTIGATION BY MEDICAL EXAMINER OR CORONER

Any person or official required to report under this Act who has reasonable cause to suspect that a child has died as a result of child abuse or neglect shall report his suspicion to the appropriate medical examiner or coroner. Any other person who has reasonable cause to suspect that a child has died as a result of child abuse or neglect may report his suspicion to the appropriate medical examiner or coroner. The medical examiner or coroner shall investigate the report and submit his findings, in writing, to the local law enforcement agency, the appropriate district attorney, the local child protective service, and, if the institution making the report is a hospital, the hospital.

SECTION 8. PHOTOGRAPHS AND X-RAYS

Any person or official required to report under this Act may take, or cause to be taken, photographs of the areas of trauma visible on a child who is the subject of a report and, if medically indicated, cause to be performed a radiological examination of the child without the consent of the child's parents or guardians. Whenever such person is required to report in his capacity as a member of the staff of a medical or other public or private institution, school, facility, or agency, he shall immediately notify the person in charge, or his designated agent, who shall then take or cause to be taken color photographs of visible trauma and shall, if medically indicated; cause to be performed a radiological examination of the child. The reasonable cost of photographs or x-rays taken under this section shall be reimbursed by the appropriate local child protective service. All photographs and x-rays taken, or copies of them, shall be sent to the local child protective service at the time the written confirmation report is sent, or as soon thereafter as possible.

SECTION 9. PROTECTIVE CUSTODY

(a) A police or law enforcement official [*a designated worker of a child protective service,*]* and a physician treating a child may take a child into protective custody without the consent of parents, guardians, or others exercising temporary or permanent control over the child when (1) he has reasonable cause

---

*As appropriate.

to believe that there exists an imminent danger to the child's life or safety, (2) the parents are unavailable or do not consent to the child's removal from their custody, and (3) there is not time to apply for a court order.

(b) The person in charge of any hospital or similar medical institution may retain custody of a child reasonably suspected of being abused or neglected, when he believes the facts so warrant, whether or not additional medical treatment is required and whether or not the parents or other person responsible for the child's welfare request the child's return.

(c) The child shall be taken to a place previously designated for this purpose by the juvenile court [*or family court or similar civil court*]* [*the local protective service*].† Such place may include a foster home; group home; shelter; hospital, if the child is or will be presently admitted to the hospital; or other institution; but it shall not be a jail or other place for the detention of criminal or juvenile offenders.

(d) No child shall be kept in protective custody under this Act for more than twenty-four hours unless authorized by a judge of a court of record.

(e) Any person taking a child into protective custody shall immediately notify the appropriate local child protective service. Upon such notification, the service shall immediately see to the protection of any other children in the home, commence a child protective investigation in accordance with Section 16 of this Act, and make every reasonable effort to inform the parent or other person responsible for the child's welfare of the place to which the child has been taken. The service shall make a reasonable attempt to return the child to his home, whenever it seems safe to do so. At the next regular session of the juvenile court [*or family court or similar civil court*]‡, the service shall (i) commence a child protection proceeding in the court, or (ii) recommend to the court [*court intake service or other initiating authority*]§ that one not be commenced. The court may order

*As appropriate.
†Optional.
‡As appropriate.
§Optional.

the commencement of a proceeding even if the service recommends against doing so, if it finds that such a proceeding would be in the best interests of the child. If a proceeding is commenced, the service shall recommend whether or not the child should be returned to his parents or other person responsible for his welfare pending further court action.

SECTION 10. IMMUNITY FROM LIABILITY

Any person, official, or institution participating in good faith in any act authorized or required by this Act shall be immune from any civil or criminal liability which might otherwise result by reason of such action.

SECTION 11. ABROGATION OF PRIVILEGED COMMUNICATIONS

The privileged quality of communication between husband and wife and any professional person and his patient or client, except that between attorney and client, shall not apply to situations involving known or suspected child abuse or neglect and shall not constitute grounds for failure to report as required or permitted by this Act, failure to cooperate with the child protective service in its activities pursuant to this Act, or failure to give or accept evidence in any judicial proceeding relating to child abuse or neglect.

SECTION 12. PENALTIES FOR FAILURE TO REPORT OR ACT

Any person, official, or institution required by this Act to report known or suspected child abuse or neglect, or required to perform any other act, who knowingly and willfully fails to do so or who knowingly and willfully prevents another person acting reasonably from doing so shall be guilty of a misdemeanor and shall be civilly liable for the damages proximately caused by such failure or prevention.

SECTION 13. INITIAL REPORTING
PROCEDURE; STATEWIDE TOLL-FREE
TELEPHONE NUMBER

(a) All reports of known or suspected child abuse or neglect made pursuant to this Act shall be made immediately by telephone to the statewide child protection center on the single, statewide, toll-free telephone number established by this Act.* They shall then be immediately transmitted to the appropriate local child protective service, unless the appropriate local plan for child protective services† provides that oral reports should be made directly to the local child protective service.

(b) All reports made pursuant to this Act shall be confirmed in writing to the appropriate local child protective service on forms supplied by the state department within forty-eight hours of the initial telephone report. The local child protective service shall send to the state center copies of all written confirmation reports it receives within twenty-four hours of receipt, regardless of where the initial oral report was received. Written confirmation reports from persons not required to report by this Act may be dispensed with by the state department for good cause shown. Written reports from persons or officials required by this Act to report shall be admissible in evidence in any judicial proceeding relating to child abuse or neglect.

(c) Reports involving known or suspected institutional child abuse or neglect shall be made and received in the same manner as all other reports made pursuant to this Act.

Title III. Local Responsibilities

SECTION 14. DESIGNATION OF LOCAL AGENCY

In each county [*or comparable political subdivision or geographic area*] of the state, the local agency having prime responsibility for local efforts to strengthen and improve the

---

*See Section 21(b), *infra.*
†*See* Subsection 16(c) and Section 18, *infra.*

prevention, identification, and treatment of child abuse and neglect shall be [*the local department of social services*] or [*a designated unit within the department, such as the child welfare service or a unified child protective service*] [*designated by the state department*] or [*designated by the appropriate local governing authority.*]

SECTION 15. POWERS, FUNCTIONS, AND DUTIES OF LOCAL AGENCY

(a) The local agency shall administer the child protective service and shall have prime local responsibility for strengthening and improving child abuse and neglect prevention and treatment efforts. To the fullest extent feasible, the local agency shall (i) encourage the cooperation and assistance of public, private, and parental organizations; (ii) serve as a local clearinghouse on programs and organizations providing or concerned with human services related to the prevention, identification, or treatment of child abuse or neglect; (iii) compile, publish, and disseminate public, professional, and staff educational and training materials and it shall provide training and technical assistance to appropriate local agencies, organizations, and individuals, either directly or indirectly; and (iv) seek and encourage the development of improved or additional programs and activities, the assumption of prevention and treatment responsibilities by additional agencies and organizations, and the coordination of existing programs and activities.

(b) Each local agency shall establish or designate a unit to act as the local child protective service to perform only those functions assigned to it by this Act and other laws, or that would further the purposes of this Act. The local child protective service shall have sufficient staff or sufficient qualifications to fulfill the purposes of this Act and shall be organized to maximize the continuity of responsibility, care, and service of individual workers toward individual children and families. In counties [*or comparable political subdivisions or geographic areas*] of sufficient size, the child protective service shall be a separate organizational unit singly administered and supervised within the local agency.

(c) To effectuate the purposes of this Act, the local agency, to the fullest extent feasible, shall cooperate with and shall seek the cooperation and involvement of all appropriate public and private agencies, including law enforcement agencies, courts of competent jurisdiction, and agencies, organizations, or programs providing or concerned with human services related to the prevention, identification, or treatment of child abuse or neglect. Such cooperation and involvement shall include joint consultation and services, joint planning, joint case management, joint public education and information services, utilization of each others' facilities, joint staff development and other training, and the creation of multi-disciplinary case diagnostic, case handling, case management, and policy planning teams.*

(d) In the furtherance of its responsibilities under this Act and in accordance with the terms and conditions of the local plan for child protective services,† the local agency may purchase and utilize the services of any public or private agency if adequate provision is made for continuity of care and accountability. When services are purchased by the local agency pursuant to this Act, their cost shall be reimbursed by the state to the locality in the same manner and to the same extent as if the services were provided directly by the local agency.‡

(e) The local agency shall have such other powers, functions, and duties as are assigned to it by this Act, other laws, and administrative procedures.

SECTION 16. THE LOCAL CHILD PROTECTIVE SERVICE

(a) The local child protective service shall be capable of receiving reports of known or suspected child abuse or neglect twenty-four hours a day, seven days a week. If it appears that the immediate safety or well-being of a child is endangered, the

---

*See section 16(e), *infra.*
†See section 18, *infra.*
‡This last sentence is not necessary if the local agency is a local office of a state administered social services department.

family may flee or the child disappear, or the facts otherwise so warrant, the child protective service shall commence an investigation immediately, regardless of the time of day or night. In all other cases, a child protective investigation shall be commenced within twenty-four hours of receipt of the report. To fulfill the requirements of this section, the child protective service shall have the capability of providing or arranging for comprehensive emergency services to children and families at all times of the day or night.

(b) For each report it receives, the child protective service shall promptly perform an appropriately thorough child protective investigation to: (i) determine the composition of the family or household, including the name, address, age, sex, and race of each child named in the report, and any siblings or other children in the same household or in the care of the same adults, the parents or other persons responsible for their welfare, and any other adults in the same household; (ii) determine whether there is probable cause to believe that any child in the family or household is abused or neglected, including a determination of harm or threatened harm to each child, the nature and extent of present or prior injuries, abuse or neglect, and any evidence thereof, and a determination of the person or persons apparently responsible for the abuse or neglect; (iii) determine the immediate or long-term risk to each child if it remains in the existing home environment; and (iv) determine the protective, treatment, and ameliorative services that appear necessary to help prevent further child abuse or neglect and to improve the home environment and the parent's ability to adequately care for the children. The purpose of the child protective investigation shall be to provide immediate and long-term protective services to prevent further abuse or neglect and to provide, or arrange for, and coordinate and monitor treatment and ameliorative services necessary to safeguard and insure the child's well-being and development and, if possible, to preserve and stabilize family life.

(c) In counties where the local plan for child protective services provides that reports of known and suspected child abuse and neglect are to be made directly to the local child protective service, the local service shall operate the telephone facility in a manner consistent with that of the statewide child protection center. Specifically, the local telephone facility shall make reports to and receive reports from the statewide center, shall immediately obtain information concerning prior reports from the statewide center and make such information available to those authorized by this Act to have it, and shall refer self-reports or inappropriate reports to appropriate community resources or agencies. The local telephone facility shall have sufficient staff of sufficient qualifications and sufficient telephonic facilities to fulfill the purposes and functions assigned to it by this Act, other laws, or administrative procedures.

(d) If the local plan for child protective services so authorizes, the child protective service may waive a full child protective investigation of reports made by agencies or individuals specified in the local plan if, after an appropriate assessment of the situation, it is satisfied that (i) the protective and service needs of the child and the family can be met by the agency or individual, (ii) the agency or individual agrees to attempt to do so, and (iii) suitable safeguards are established and observed. Suitable safeguards shall include a written agreement from the agency or individual to report periodically on the status of the family, a written agreement to report immediately to the local service at any time that the child's safety or well-being is threatened despite the agency's or individual's efforts, and periodic monitoring of the agency's or individual's efforts by the local service for a reasonable period of time.

(e) The child protective service shall convene one or more interdisciplinary "Child Protection Teams" to assist it in its diagnostic, assessment, service, and coordination responsibilities. The head of the child protective service* or his designee shall serve as the team's coordinator. Members of the team shall serve at the coordinator's invitation and shall include representatives of appropriate health, mental health, social service, and law enforcement agencies.

(f) If the local child protective service is denied reasonable

---

*In areas in which there is not a separate child protective service, this sentence should begin: "The head of the local agency . . ."

access to a child by the parents or other persons and the local service deems that the best interests of the child so require, it shall seek an appropriate court order or other legal authority to examine and interview such child.

(g) If the child protective service determines that a child requires immediate or long term protection, either (1) through homemaker care, day care, casework supervison, or other services to stabilize the home environment, or (2) through foster care, shelter care, or other substitute care to remove the child from his parent's custody, such services first shall be offered for the voluntary acceptance of the parent or other person responsible for the child's welfare. If such services are refused and the child protective service deems that the best interests of the child so require, the service shall seek an appropriate court order or other legal authority to protect the child.*

(h) After providing for the immediate protection of the child but prior to offering any services to a family, the child protective service shall forthwith notify the adult subjects of the report, in writing, of the existence of the report and their rights pursuant to this Act, including their right to refuse services and their right to obtain access to and amend, expunge, or remove reports in the central register of child protection cases. The service shall explain that it has no legal authority to compel the family to accept services; however, it may inform the family of the obligations and authority of the child protective service to petition the juvenile court to decide whether a child is in need of care and protection or to refer the case to the police, district attorney or criminal court.

(i) No later than sixty days after receiving the initial report, the child protective service shall determine whether the report is unfounded or not and report its findings forthwith to the central register on a form supplied by the state department; however, the statewide center may extend the period in which such determinations must be made in individual cases for up to thirty days, but such extensions shall only be made once and only upon good cause shown.

---

*The police and, if authorized by the optional provision in section 9(a), the child protective service may take the child into protective custody.

(j) If the local child protective service determines that there is not probable cause to believe that a child is abused or neglected, it shall close its protective case. However, if it appears that the child or family could benefit from other social services, the local service may suggest such services for the family's voluntary acceptance or refusal. If the family declines such services, the local service shall take no further action.

(k) If the local child protective service determines that there is probable cause to believe that a child is abused or neglected, based upon its determination of the protective, treatment, and ameliorative service needs of the child and family, the local service shall develop, with the family, an appropriate service plan for the family's voluntary acceptance or refusal. The local service shall comply with subsection (h) by explaining its lack of legal authority to compel the acceptance of services and may explain its concomitant authority to petition the juvenile court or refer the case to the police, district attorney, or criminal court.

(l) If the local child protective service determines that the best interests of a child require juvenile court or criminal court action because an appropriate service plan was rejected or because of any other appropriate reason, the local service may initiate a court proceeding or a referral to the appropriate court related service, police department, district attorney, or any combination thereof.

(m) The child protective service shall give telephone notice and immediately forward a copy of reports which involve the death of a child to the appropriate district attorney [or other appropriate law enforcement agency] and medical examiner or coroner. In addition, upon the prior written request of the district attorney or if the local service otherwise deems it appropriate, a copy of any or all reports made pursuant to this Act which allege criminal conduct shall be forwarded immediately by the child protective service to the appropriate district attorney.

(n) If a law enforcement investigation is also contemplated or is in progress, the child protective service shall attempt to coordinate its efforts and concerns with those of the law enforcement agency.

(o) In any juvenile or criminal court proceeding commenced by the child protective service or by any other individual or agency, the service shall assist the court during all stages of the court proceeding in accordance with the purposes of this Act, the juvenile court act, and the penal law.

(p) The local child protective service shall maintain a local child abuse and neglect index of all cases reported under this Act which can enable it to determine the location of case records and to monitor the timely and proper investigation and disposition of cases. The index shall include the information contained in the initial, progress, and final reports required under this Act, and any other appropriate information.

(q) The child protective service shall prepare and transmit to the statewide child protection center the initial, preliminary, progress, and final reports required by section 21 (e) of this Act.

(r) The child protective service may request and shall receive from any agency of the state, or any of its political subdivisions, and any other agency providing services under the local plan for child protective services such cooperation, assistance, and information as will enable it to fulfill its responsibilities under this section.

SECTION 17. THE COMMUNITY CHILD PROTECTION ADVISORY BOARD

(a) The appropriate local chief executive officer shall convene a "community child protection advisory board." Members of the board shall include representatives of local law enforcement agencies, the juvenile [or family] court, appropriate public, private, and parental organizations, and individuals of distinction in human services, law, and community life, broadly representative of all social and economic groups. The board shall have no less than five and no more than fifteen members, of which at least twenty percent shall be individuals of distinction not otherwise representing a public, private, or parental organization or group.

(b) The community child protection advisory board, both

independently and in conjunction with the local agency and the local child protective service, shall assist in local efforts to improve the prevention, identification, and treatment of child abuse and neglect. The advisory board may meet at any time to consider any issue in relation to child abuse and neglect, may confer with any individuals, groups, and agencies, and may issue reports or recommendations on any subject it deems appropriate.

SECTION 18. THE LOCAL PLAN FOR CHILD PROTECTIVE SERVICES

(a) After consultation with the community child protection advisory board, local law enforcement agencies, the juvenile [or family or other similar civil] court, other relevant public, private, and parental organizations, and individuals of distinction in human services, law and community life, broadly representative of all social and economic sectors, each local agency shall prepare a local plan for child protective services every two years, to be approved by the community child protection advisory board and the state department.

(b) The local plan shall describe the local agency's implementation of this Act, including (i) the child protective service's organization, staffing, method of operations, and financing, (ii) the programs in effect or planned in connection with the enforcement or implementation of this Act and other child abuse and neglect laws, and (iii) the terms and conditions under which the local child protective service may waive a full child protective investigation pursuant to subsection 16 (d) of this Act.

(c) The plan may take effect no sooner than 90 days and no later than 150 days after its submission to the state department. The date of submission shall be determined by the state department, which may stagger the receipt of such plans throughout the year.

(d) A public hearing shall be held by the community child protection advisory board at least 30 days before the plan must be submitted to the state department for its approval or disapproval. The plan shall be made available to the public for review and comment for at least 60 days before the public hearing. The availability of the plan and the hearing shall be widely publicized within the county [or comparable political or geographic subdivisions.]

(e) The plan shall be submitted to the state department after approval by the community child protection advisory board or upon the certification of the local agency that, after all reasonable efforts, the local agency and the board were not able to develop a mutually agreeable plan, stating the reasons therefore. The board may append to any plan it does not approve a statement of its reasons for disapproval before it is submitted to the state department.

(f) Within 30 days of its receipt, the state department shall certify whether or not the local plan fulfills the purposes and the requirements of this Act. If it disapproves the local plan, the state department shall give the reasons therefore, in writing, and the local agency shall have forty-five days to submit an amended plan in compliance with subsections (a) and (e) of this section. The state department shall have thirty days to certify whether or not the amended plan fulfills the purposes and meets the requirements of this Act. If the state department again disapproves the plan, the local agency shall have an additional thirty days to submit an amended plan of its own. The state department shall have thirty days to certify whether or not the second amended plan fulfills the purposes and meets the requirements of this Act. If the state department again disapproves the plan, at any time thereafter, it may withhold state reimbursement for all or part of the local agency's activities. The state department's failure to certify approval or disapproval of a plan within the times set forth in this section shall be deemed an approval. Decisions of the state department under this section shall be subject to judicial review in the form and manner prescribed by the state civil procedure law.*

---

*The last two sentences of this section would be inappropriate in States in which the local child protection program is state administered.

Title IV. State Responsibilities

SECTION 19. DESIGNATION
OF STATE DEPARTMENT

The state department having prime responsibility for state efforts to strengthen and improve the prevention, identification, and treatment of child abuse and neglect shall be the State Department of ―――――――――― .

SECTION 20. POWERS, FUNCTIONS,
AND DUTIES OF THE STATE DEPARTMENT

(a) The state department shall serve as a state clearinghouse on programs and groups providing or concerned with human services related to the prevention, identification, or treatment of child abuse or neglect. It shall compile, publish, and disseminate public, professional, and staff educational and training materials and provide training and technical assistance, directly or indirectly. The department shall encourage the development of improved and additional state and local programs and activities; encourage the assumption of prevention and treatment responsibilities by additional agencies and groups; encourage the coordination of existing programs and activities; and conduct, support, or foster research and demonstration projects.

(b) The head of the state department shall convene a "state child abuse and neglect coordinating committee," to coordinate and assist state efforts to strengthen and improve child abuse and neglect prevention and treatment. The committee shall be chaired by the head of the state department, or his personal designee, and shall be composed of representatives from state agencies providing or concerned with human services related to the prevention, identification, or treatment of child abuse and neglect.

(c) At least 45 days before the beginning of the state's fiscal year, the state department shall prepare and transmit to the Governor and the Legislature an "annual state report on child abuse and neglect prevention and treatment." The annual report shall describe the specific measures adopted to implement the provisions of this Act, as well as the accomplishments and shortcomings of state and local efforts to prevent and treat child abuse and neglect. The report shall include a full statistical analysis of the status and outcome of cases reported to the statewide center, an evaluation of services offered to the children and families reported, its recommendations for additional legislation or services to fulfill the purposes of this Act, and any other information deemed relevant. Based upon materials prepared by the state department pursuant to Title XX of the Federal Social Security Act and Public Law 93-247, the annual report shall describe state and local efforts to develop, strengthen, and carry out child abuse and neglect efforts in the coming year. The annual report shall also include a section prepared by the statewide citizen's committee on child abuse and neglect* which contains its comments, recommendations, or any other information deemed relevant to child abuse and neglect prevention and treatment efforts.

(d) The state department shall adopt regulations and forms necessary to implement this Act upon 45 days public notice for review and comment. However, this period may be shortened if the head of the state department certifies, in writing, the existence of an urgent necessity to do so and gives the reason therefore.

(e) The state department may request and shall receive from any agency of the state, or any of its political subdivisions, any agency receiving public funds, or any other agency providing services under the local child protective services plan, such cooperation, assistance, and information as will enable the state department and local agencies to fulfill their responsibilities under this Act.

(f) The state department shall have such other powers, functions, and duties as are assigned to it by this Act, other laws, and administrative procedures.

---

*See section 22, *infra.*

SECTION 21. THE STATEWIDE CHILD
PROTECTION CENTER AND THE CENTRAL REGISTER
OF CHILD PROTECTION CASES

(a) The state department shall establish a "statewide child protection center." The center shall be a separate organizational unit, singly administered and supervised within the state department, with sufficient staff of sufficient qualifications and sufficient resources, including telephone facilities, to fulfill the purposes and functions assigned to it by this Act, other laws, or administrative procedures.

(b) There shall be a single statewide, toll-free telephone number within the statewide child protection center which all persons, whether or not mandated by law, may use to report known or suspected child abuse or neglect at any hour of the day or night, on any day of the week. Immediately upon receipt of such reports, the center shall transmit the contents of the report, either orally or electronically, to the appropriate local child protective agency. Any person or family seeking assistance in meeting child care responsibilities may use the statewide telephone number to obtain assistance or information in accordance with section 3 of this Act. Any other person may use the statewide number to obtain assistance or information concerning the handling of child protection cases.

(c) There shall be a central register of child protection cases maintained in the statewide center. Through the recording of initial, preliminary, progress, and final reports, the central register shall be operated in such a manner as to enable the center to: (i) immediately identify and locate prior reports or cases of child abuse or neglect; (ii) continuously monitor the current status of all child protection cases;* and (iii) regularly evaluate the effectiveness and existing laws and programs through the development and analysis of statistical and other information.

(d) Immediately upon receiving an oral or written report of known or suspected child abuse or neglect, the statewide center shall notify the local service of a previous report concerning a

---

*Optional, because the costs of receiving, recording, and monitoring progress reports may be beyond the resources of some states.

subject of the present report or other pertinent information. In addition, upon satisfactory identification procedures, to be established by regulation of the state department, any person or official legally authorized to have access to records relating to child abuse and neglect may request and shall be immediately provided the information requested in accordance with the requirements of this Act. However, no information shall be released unless it prominently states whether the report is "under investigation," "unfounded," "under care," or "closed," whichever the case may be. The names and other identifying data and the dates and the circumstances of any persons requesting or receiving information from the central register shall be entered in the register record.

(e) (i) The statewide center shall prepare, print, and distribute initial, preliminary, progress, and final reporting forms to each local child protective service. (ii) Initial written reports from the reporting source shall contain the following information to the extent known at the time the report is made: the names and addresses of the child and his parents or other persons responsible for his welfare; the child's age, sex and race; the nature and extent of the child's abuse or neglect, including any evidence of prior injuries, abuse, or neglect of the child or his siblings; the names of the persons apparently responsible for the abuse or neglect; family composition, including names, ages, sexes, and races of other children in the home; the name of the person making the report, his occupation, and where he can be reached; the actions taken by the reporting source, including the taking of photographs and x-rays, placing the child in protective custody, or notifying the medical examiner or coroner; and any other information the person making the report believes might be helpful in the furtherance of the purposes of this Act. (iii) Preliminary reports from the local child protective service shall be made no later than seven days after receipt of an initial report and shall describe the status of the child protective investigation up to that time, including an evaluation of the present family situation and danger to the child or children, corrections or updating of the initial report, and actions taken or contemplated. (iv) Progress reports* from the local service shall be made at such regular intervals as the regulations of the state department establish, and shall describe the child protective services' plan for protective, treatment, or ameliorative services and the services accepted or refused by the family. (v) Final reports from the local service shall be made no later than 14 days after a case is determined to be unfounded or is closed for other reasons and shall describe the final disposition of the case, including an evaluation of the reasons and circumstances surrounding the close of the case and the unmet needs of the child or family, and the causes thereof, including the unavailability or unsuitability of existing services, and the need for additional services.† (vi) The foregoing reports may contain such additional information in the furtherance of the purposes of this Act as the state department, by regulation, may require. (vii) All of the foregoing reports shall also be required of the child protective service in cases in which the local service foregoes a full protective investigation pursuant to the local plan for child protective services and subsection 16 (d) of this Act. (viii) For good cause shown, the local service may amend any report previously sent to the statewide center. (ix) Unless otherwise prescribed by this Act, the contents, form, manner, and timing of making the foregoing reports shall be established by regulation of the state department.

(f) All cases in the central register shall be classified in one of four categories: "under investigation," "unfounded," "under care," or "closed," whichever the case may be. All information identifying the subjects of an unfounded report shall be expunged from the register forthwith. Identifying information on all other records shall be removed from the register no later than five years after the case is closed. However, if another report is received involving the same child, his sibling or offspring, or a child in the care of the same adults, the identifying information may be maintained in the register until five years

---

*Progress reports are considered optional because the cost of operating a system to store and monitor them may be beyond the resources of some states.

†But *see* section 16(j), *supra,* which authorizes the child protective service to provide services to the child or family if they are otherwise in need of such services and voluntarily accept them.

after the subsequent case or report is closed.

(g) The central register may contain such other information which the state department determines to be in furtherance of the purposes of this Act. At any time, the statewide center may amend, expunge, or remove from the central register any record upon good cause shown and upon notice to the subjects of the report and the local child protective service.

(h) Upon request, a subject of a report shall be entitled to receive a copy of all information contained in the central register pertaining to his case. Provided, however, that the statewide center is authorized to prohibit the release of data that would identify a person who, in good faith, made a report or cooperated in a subsequent investigation, when it reasonably finds that disclosure of such information would be likely to be detrimental to the safety or interests of such person; in addition, the center may seek a court order from a court of competent jurisdiction prohibiting the release of any information which the court finds is likely to be harmful to the subject of the report.

(i) At any time subsequent to the completion of the investigation, but in no event later than sixty days after receipt of the report, at which time this Act contemplates that the investigation will have been completed, a subject of a report may request the state department to amend, expunge, or remove the record of the report from the register. If the state department refuses to do so or does not act within thirty days, the subject shall have the right to a fair hearing within the state department to determine whether the record of the report should be amended, expunged, or removed on the grounds that it is inaccurate or it is being maintained in a manner inconsistent with this Act. Such fair hearing shall be held within a reasonable time after the subject's request at a reasonable place and hour. The appropriate local child protective service shall be given notice of the fair hearing. In such hearings, the burden of providing the accuracy and consistency of the record shall be on the state department and the appropriate local child protective service. A juvenile court [*family court or similar civil court*] finding of child abuse or child neglect shall be presumptive evidence that the report was not unfounded. The hearing shall be conducted by the head of the state department or his designated agent, who is hereby authorized and empowered to order the amendment, expunction, or removal of the record to make it accurate or consistent with the requirements of this Act. The decision shall be made, in writing, at the close of the hearing, or within thirty days thereof, and shall state the reasons upon which it is based. Decisions of the state department under this section shall be subject to judicial review in the form and manner prescribed by the state civil procedure law.

(j) To the fullest extent possible, written notice of any amendment, expunction, or removal of any record made pursuant to this Act shall be served upon each subject of such report and the appropriate local child protective service. The service, upon receipt of such notice, shall take the appropriate similar action in regard to the local child abuse and neglect index and shall inform, for the same purpose, any other individuals or agencies which received such record pursuant to this Act or in any other manner. Nothing in this section is intended to require the destruction of case records.

SECTION 22. STATEWIDE CITIZEN'S COMMITTEE ON CHILD ABUSE AND NEGLECT

The Governor shall appoint the chairperson and members of a "statewide citizen's committee on child abuse and neglect" to consult with and advise the Governor, the state department, and the state child abuse and neglect coordinating committee. The committee shall be composed of individuals of distinction in human services, law, and community life, broadly representative of all social and economic communities across the state, who shall be appointed to three year staggered terms. The chairperson and members of the committee shall serve without compensation, although their travel and per diem expenses shall be reimbursed in accordance with standard state procedures. Under procedures adopted by the committee, it may meet at any time, confer with any individuals, groups, and agencies;

and may issue reports or recommendations on any aspect of child abuse or neglect it deems appropriate.

Title V: General

SECTION 23. REPORTS OF INSTITUTIONAL CHILD ABUSE AND NEGLECT

(a) Through written agreement, the state department shall designate the public or private agency or agencies responsible for investigating reports involving known or suspected institutional child abuse or neglect. The designated agency or agencies must be other than and separately administered from the one involved in the alleged acts or omissions. Subject to the preceeding limitation, the agency may be the state department, the local child protective service, a law enforcement agency, or another appropriate agency.

(b) The agreement shall describe the specific terms and conditions of the designation, including the manner in which reports of known or suspected institutional child abuse or neglect will be received through the single statewide telephone number, the manner in which such reports will be investigated, the remedial action which will be taken, and the manner in which the statewide child protection center will be kept fully informed of the progress, findings, and disposition of the investigation.

SECTION 24. CONFIDENTIALITY OF REPORTS AND RECORDS

(a) In order to protect the rights of the child, his parents, or guardians, all records concerning reports of non-institutional child abuse and neglect, including reports made to the state department, state center, state central register, local child protective services, and all records generated as a result of such reports, shall be confidential and shall not be disclosed except as specifically authorized by this Act or other applicable law. It shall be a misdemeanor to permit, assist, or encourage the unauthorized release of any information contained in such reports or records.

(b) No person, official, or agency shall have access to such records unless in furtherance of the purposes directly connected with the administration of this Act. Such persons, officials, agencies, and purposes for access include:

(i) a local child protective service in the furtherance of its responsibilities under this Act;

(ii) a police or law enforcement agency investigating a report of known or suspected child abuse or neglect;

(iii) a physician who has before him a child whom he reasonably suspects may be abused or neglected;

(iv) a person legally authorized to place a child in protective custody when such person requires the information in the report or record to determine whether to place the child in protective custody;

(v) an agency having the legal responsibility or authorization to care for, treat, or supervise a child or parent, guardian, or other person responsible for the child's welfare who is the subject of a report;

(vi) except in regard to harmful or detrimental information as provided in section 21(h), any subject of the report; if the subject of the report is a minor or is otherwise legally incompetent, his general guardian or guardian *ad litem;*

(vii) a court, upon its finding that access to such records may be necessary for the determination of an issue before such court; however, such access shall be limited to in camera inspection, unless the court determines that public disclosure of the information contained therein is necessary for the resolution of an issue then pending before it;

(viii) a grand jury, upon its determination that access to such records is necessary in the conduct of its official business;

(ix) any appropriate state or local official responsible for administration, supervision, or legislation in relation to the prevention or treatment of child abuse or neglect when carrying out his official functions;

(x) any person engaged in bona fide research purposes; provided, however, that no information identifying the subjects of the report shall be made available to the researcher unless it is absolutely essential to the research purpose, suitable provision is made to maintain the confidentiality of the data, and the head of the state department or local agency gives prior written approval.

(c) Upon request, a physician or the person in charge of an institution, school, facility or agency making a legally mandated report shall receive a summary of the findings of and actions taken by the local child protective service in response to his report. The amount of detail such summary contains shall depend on the source of the report and shall be established by regulations of the state department. Any other person making a report shall be entitled to learn the general disposition of such report.

(d) A person given access to the names or other information identifying the subjects of the report, except the subject of the report, shall not make public such identifying information unless he is a district attorney or other law enforcement official and the purpose is to initiate court action. Violation of this subsection shall be a misdemeanor.

(e) Nothing in this Act is intended to affect existing policies or procedures concerning the status of court and criminal justice system records.

SECTION 25. RIGHT TO REPRESENTATION IN COURT PROCEEDINGS

(a) Any child who is alleged to be abused or neglected in a juvenile court [*family or other similar civil court*] proceeding shall have independent legal representation in such proceeding. If independent legal representation is not available, the court shall appoint counsel to represent the child at public expense.

The attorney representing a child under this section shall also serve as the child's guardian *ad litem* unless a guardian *ad litem* has been appointed by the appropriate court.

(b) Any parent or other person responsible for a child's welfare alleged to have abused or neglected a child in a civil or criminal proceeding shall be entitled to legal representation in such proceeding. If he is unable to afford such representation, the appropriate court shall appoint counsel to represent him at public expense.

(c) In every juvenile [*or family*] court proceeding concerning alleged child abuse or neglect in which it is a party, the local child protective service shall have the assistance of legal counsel [*provided by the local civil law officer of the appropriate county or comparable political subdivision or geographic area.*]

SECTION 26. EDUCATION AND TRAINING

Within the appropriation available, the state department and the local agency, both jointly and individually, shall conduct a continuing education and training program for state and local department staff, persons and officials required to report, the general public, and any other appropriate persons. The program shall be designed to encourage the fullest degree of reporting of known and suspected child abuse and neglect, including institutional abuse and neglect, and to improve communication, cooperation, and coordination among all agencies in the identification, prevention, and treatment of child abuse and neglect. The program shall inform the general public and professionals of the nature and extent of child abuse and neglect and of their responsibilities, obligations, powers, and immunity from liability under this Act. It should also include information on the diagnosis of child abuse and neglect and the roles and procedures of the local child protective service and the community child protection team, the statewide child protection center and central register, the juvenile court and of the protective, treatment, and ameliorative services available to children and their families. The program should also encourage parents and other persons having responsibility for the welfare of children to seek assistance on their own in meeting their child care responsibilities and encourage the voluntary acceptance of available services when they are needed. It should also include wide publicity and dissemination of information on the existence and number of the twenty-four hour, state-wide, toll-free telephone service to assist persons seeking assistance and to receive reports of known and suspected abuse and neglect.

SECTION 27. SEPARABILITY

If any provision of this Act or the application thereof to any person or circumstances is held to be invalid, the remainder of the Act and the application of such provision to other persons or circumstances shall not be affected thereby.

SECTION 28. AUTHORIZATION FOR APPROPRIATIONS

There are hereby authorized to be appropriated such sums as may be necessary to effectuate the purposes of this Act.

SECTION 29. EFFECTIVE DATE

This Act shall take effect on _____ .

10
CASE REPORTS

CASE 1: The patient was born prematurely after six months' gestation. At the age of one year, she was taken to a hospital emergency room with a history of having fallen out of her crib. X-ray study revealed fractures of the right and left wrists. She was not admitted to the hospital at that time. Several weeks later, the mother took her to another hospital where she stated that she tripped with the baby and noted swelling on the ankles. Fractured right and left ankles were noted on x-ray examination.

Two months later, the patient was admitted to a third hospital with a fractured left arm and signs of malnutrition. X-ray study at the hospital revealed healed old fractures as well as the newly incurred fracture of the left humerus.

The case was referred to social service workers, who, after investigation, reported the parent's denial of having inflicted trauma and considered the home environment adequate. No further action was taken in view of the social service report.

At the age of two, this patient was admitted to the hospital with multiple fractures and symptoms strongly suggesting rickets or scurvy. The case was again studied by the social service section of the hospital and again the home environment was found acceptable. The Society for the Prevention of Cruelty to Children investigated the family problem to rule out physical abuse to the child. At that time, the mother stated that she was a victim of "epileptic seizures." The Society felt assured that the injuries sustained by the patient were due to trauma incurred during the mother's seizures and not to any negligence or abuse on the part of the parents. Six months later, the child was taken to the emergency room of a hospital where she was pronounced dead on arrival.

The mother stated that she had fallen down a flight of stairs with the child in her arms. At the time that the mother brought the patient into the emergency room, there were no signs of trauma on any part of her own body.

At autopsy, the following findings were noted: Subdural

hemorrhages; cerebral edema; contusions of the scalp and face; multiple abrasions of the face and extremities, with scab formation; old lacerations of the lips; and multiple contusions and abrasions of the body. A diagnosis of maltreatment was made by the medical examiner, but no legal action was taken at the time.

CASE 2: Several months later the one-month-old sibling of the patient in Case 1 was admitted to the hospital with a diagnosis of malnutrition, dehydration and possible vitamin deficiency. The patient responded well to supportive measures and was discharged in good condition.

Two weeks later examination in the pediatric follow-up clinic revealed soft-tissue swellings of the left wrist and left thigh. The patient was admitted to the hospital and x-ray study showed fractures of the distal end of the left radius and ulna. The possibility of pathologic fractures was considered, but laboratory data were all within normal limits.

Inflicted trauma was suspected and data on the medical past history of the patient and sibling were obtained. The "accidental death" report of the sibling in Case 1 prompted further investigations which confirmed the diagnosis of maltreatment in Case 2.

The parents persisted in their denials of inflicted trauma and abuse and expressed concern for the welfare of their children. The mother impressed both physicians and social service workers with her affection and care of her four children. Her clinic visits gave further evidence of her motherly affection. The children appeared well dressed, and there was no obvious indication of neglect.

In view of the past history of maltreatment in another sibling and the inadequacy of the parent's explanation of the patient's physical findings, this child was kept in the hospital to await court action. The court's decision, in view of the evidence presented, was to place the child in a foster home.

CASE 3: A six-week-old infant was admitted to the hospital because of swelling of the right thigh of four day's duration. The mother stated to the examining physician that the child had fallen from its crib and struck its right leg on the floor. X-ray examination revealed complete fracture through the midshaft of the right femur with posterior displacement of the distal fragment. The patient was in Bryant's traction for two weeks and was discharged in good condition after application of a hip spica.

A few weeks later the child was admitted to another hospital with multiple contusions and abrasions. Investigation by the social service department indicated that the father had thrown the child on the floor, shattering the cast and inflicting serious head trauma resulting in bilateral subdural hematomas. The child was recently seen in the pediatric clinic, where multiple signs of intracranial damage were noted. The child is now blind and mentally retarded.

These three cases of maltreated children are typical examples of parentally inflicted trauma. In the first case, the abuse and trauma led to the patient's death. The patient in case 2 was rescued from future maltreatment and possible death by removal of the patient from the life-threatening environment. The child was placed in a foster home waiting the rehabilitation of the parents and adjustment of the home environment. In case 3, the results of a battered child, if the patient survives, are evident. This child gives evidence of the irreversible brain damage resulting from repeatedly inflicted trauma.

These cases strongly express the possibilities facing the victim of maltreatment. The results depend on the alertness and astuteness of the medical, social and legal agents of our society.

CASE 4: This one-year-old male infant was born at term. His first admission was at the age of five months for anemia and an abscess formation of the right tibial area. There was no history or evidence of trauma on physical examination. The parents related a history that there were many insects and rodents at home. The patient had not received any immunization. There were four other siblings at home. There was no history of tuberculosis or allergies in the family.

On physical examination, the infant looked pale and acutely ill. He was in the 40th percentile for his weight. The most significant finding was the fluctuant erythematous swelling (3 x 4 centimeters) over the right tibia with tender right inguinal adenopathy.

X-rays of the anterior aspect of the right lower leg showed soft-tissue mass with no bony involvement. Incision and drainage under local anesthesia was done, and the child was discharged on the fifth hospital day with a weight gain of one-half pound.

The patient was readmitted at eight months of age for a hematoma of the left ear pinna and anemia. The parents stated that the swelling of the ear was the result of a rat bite. A detailed social service inquiry, including a home visit, was undertaken during the second admission. There were many family problems apparent in all areas of married family life. The social worker could shed no light on the cause of the child's hematoma or upon the abscess treated on the first admission.

A third admission was noted at one year of age for impetigo. Another extensive social service investigation was conducted. From the information gathered by the investigators, the medical suspicions and the physical findings, neglect on the part of the parents resulted in court action. This action was taken to protect the child from future recurring injuries. The child, by court action based on evidence presented, was placed in The New York Foundling Hospital.

CASE 5: A five-year-old male child was admitted to the hospital for multiple contusions and abrasions about the body and head secondary to trauma. The question of inflicted trauma was entertained by the examining physicians. History revealed that the mother was responsible for the maltreatment of this patient. The father and child both confirmed the fact that the mother was responsible for the periodic episodes of abuse. The child was with foster parents from age one to four years and was living with his own parents when the injuries occurred.

On physical examination, the child had multiple areas of contusions and abrasions about the face and head, chest and extremities. Skull and total body x-rays revealed no fractures. Patient was discharged to The New York Foundling Hospital and plans were made to have the child placed in a foster home.

CASE 6: An eight-year-old boy who was a ward of The New York Foundling Hospital was admitted for multiple contusions inflicted by the foster parents, as related by the child, for misbehaving at school. These periodic beatings were far beyond the normal excuses of discipline. Further questioning revealed that the foster parents would at times force the child up against a hot radiator until body burns were evident.

On physical examination, multiple contusions and ecchymosis of back and extremities were noted. Total body x-rays revealed no fractures. Patient was otherwise normal.

The child was returned to The New York Foundling Hospital for continued social service investigation and placement.

CASE 7: A three-year-old male was admitted from the emergency room with burns involving 10 to 15 percent of the body surface. According to the history, the child was placed in a bathtub and hot water was turned on accidentally.

On physical examination, his temperature was 101.80, pulse 130. The examination was essentially normal except for redness and blistering of feet, buttock, scrotum and hands.

The patient was treated with antibiotics, sedatives and open air treatment with aseptic care of the burns. X-ray of the extremities and rib cage revealed no fractures; chest film was normal. CBC, urinalysis and electrolytes repeatedly were normal. After thirty-seven days of hospitalization, the child had a good recovery from the burns.

The social service department investigated the problem in depth. Both the patient and another sibling were born out of wedlock with different fathers. At the time of the alleged accident, another male companion of the mother's was left to care for the patient. During a fit of rage, this friend of the mother's placed the child in a tub of boiling water.

The areas burned aroused the suspicions of the physicians. The perineal area and buttocks were severely burned; the hands and feet were also involved. The intervening areas of the body surface were normal. It appeared from the parts of the body burned that the child was forced to sit in the boiling water and, in the patient's attempt to protect himself, he extended his feet and hands which came into contact with the water.

Social service investigations and family unit adjustments warranted discharge of this child to his home. The physician recommended periodic visits to the Pediatric Clinic and interval visits to the home by social service.

These case reports of maltreatment in children represent only a small number of the ways that abuse and neglect can be inflicted. They also illustrate the different members or individuals in a family group who can be responsible for the willfully inflicted trauma or abuse on these children.

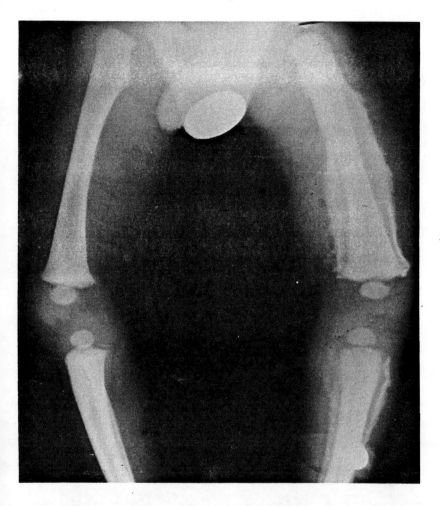

Figure 1. Female, six months old with history of thigh swelling. Film taken four to eight days after injury shows evidence of periosteal hemorrhage, metaphyseal fragmentation and periosteal reaction of femur, tibia and fibula.

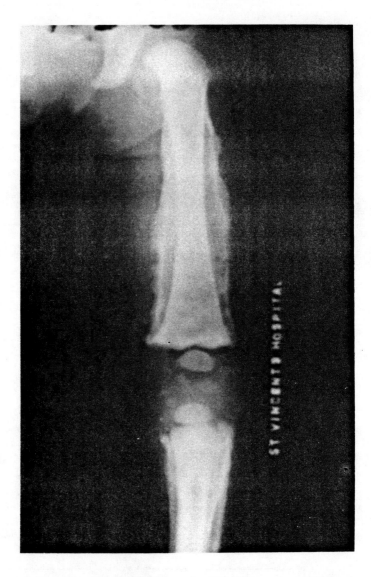

Figure 2. Female, six-and-a-half months old. Films taken four to six weeks after initial episode of inflicted trauma show extensive periosteal reaction with metaphyseal fragmentation and some calcification.

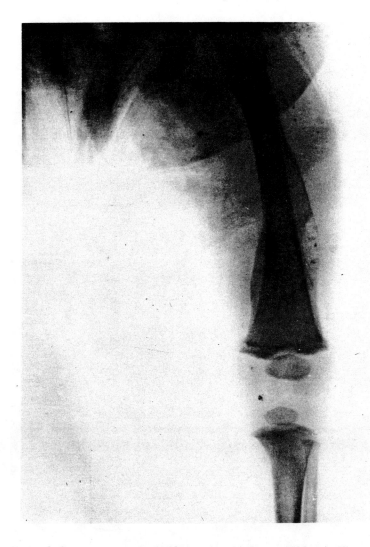

Figure 3. Female, six-and-a-half months old. Same child as in Figure 2. X-ray film taken three months later shows reparative changes, external cortical thickening, well-calcified subperiosteal reaction and squaring of the metaphysis due to new bone formation.

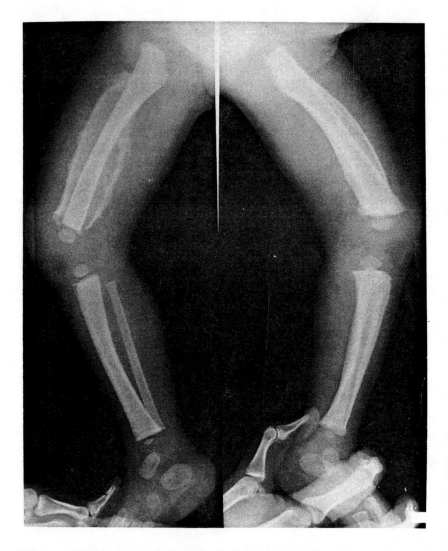

Figure 4. Male, seven months old, admitted to hospital on several occasions for "accidental" injury to thighs. The left femur shows evidence of periosteal reaction with calcification and new bone formation three to six weeks after inflicted trauma. Metaphyseal squaring also noted. The right femur in the same child shows evidence of more recently incurred injury (1-2 weeks) with subperiosteal hemorrhage, some calcification, metaphyseal fragmentation and chip fractures.

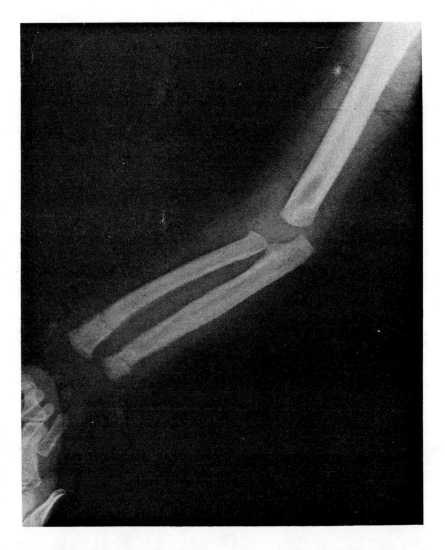

Figure 5a. Female, six-and-a-half months old, same child as in Figures 2 and 3. Inflicted injury caused x-ray evidence of fractures through distal ends of the radius and ulna.

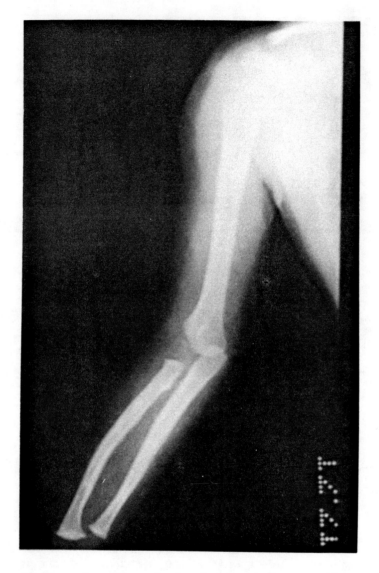

Figure 5b. X-ray taken six months after the injury indicates complete healing with no evidence of previous fractures.

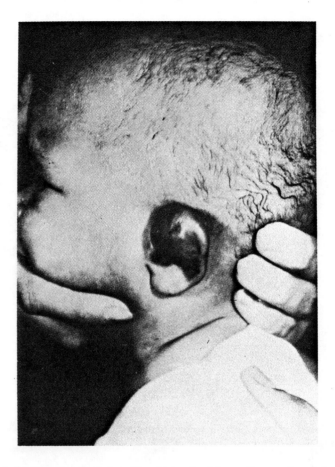

Figure 6. Male, seven months old, admitted with swollen ecchymotic painful ear attributed to insect bite, later discovered to be result of inflicted trauma with wooden instrument by one of the parents.

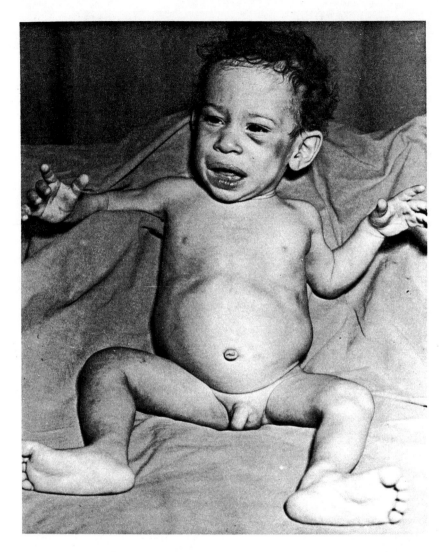

Figure 7. Male, seven months old, admitted with evidences of neglect and abuse. Child was undernourished, anemic and extremely irritable. Patient was pummeled with resultant ecchymosis around left eye and left temporal region of face. The right thigh was swollen and very tender. X-ray showed superiosteal hemorrhage and chip fractures of the right femur.

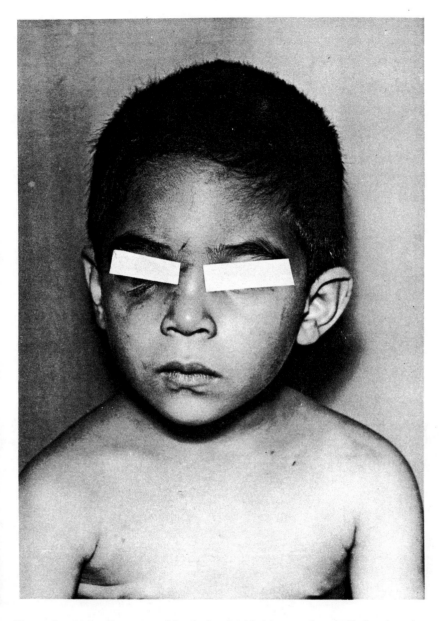

Figure 8a. Male, five years old, admitted with history of periodic beatings by parent. Physical evidence of abrasions and bruises in various stages with recent trauma to right eye and face.

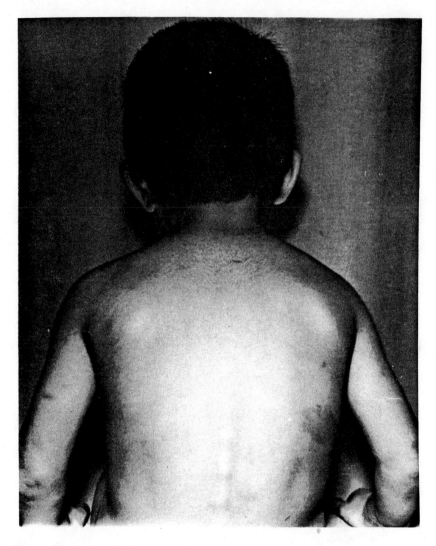

Figure 8b. Same child in posterior view showing trickling of blood behind left ear and a large associated left cephalohematoma. Scattered ecchymotic areas can also be seen on the patient's body.

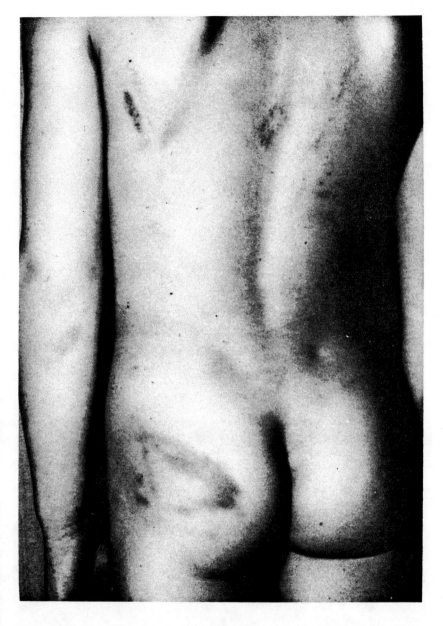

Figure 9. Male, eight-and-a-half years old. Ecchymotic areas over the body, especially on back due to inflicted injury by a sadistic parent who used belt buckles and a variety of other metal instruments.

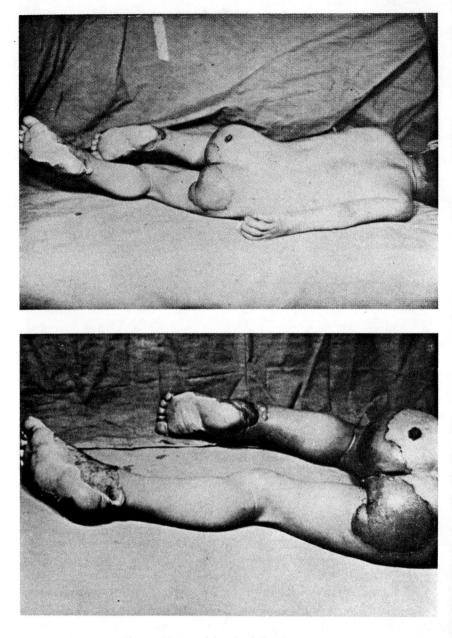

Figure 10 a and b (see following page).

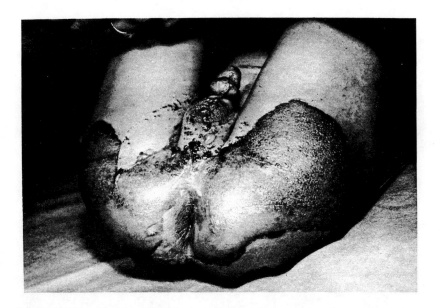

Figure 10 a, b, c. Male, three years old. Various views of burns of the buttocks, hands and feet of a child who was placed in a tub of boiling water.

Figure 11. Three female siblings abandoned by alcoholic parents. Physical examination revealed evidences of inflicted trauma, extremely poor personal and skin hygiene with associated signs of malnutrition and anemia.

REFERENCES

1. Ackerman, N. W.: Preventive implications of family research. In Caplan, Gerald (Ed.): *Prevention of Mental Disorders in Children.* New York, Basic, 1961.
2. Adelson, L.: Homicide by pepper. *J Forensic Sci, 9*:391, July 1964.
3. Adelson, L.: Homicide by starvation, the nutritional variant of the battered child. *JAMA, 186*:458, 1963.
4. Adelson, L.: Slaughter of the innocents — A study of forty-six homicides in which the victims were children. *N Engl J Med, 264*:1345, 1961.
5. Allen, A., and Morton, A.: *This is Your Child: The Story of the National Society for the Prevention of Cruelty to Children.* London, Routledge and K. Paul Ltd., 1961.
6. Altman, D. H., and Smith, R. L.: Unrecognized trauma in infants and children. *J Bone Joint Surg (Amer), 42A*:407, 1960.
7. American Academy of Pediatrics Committee on Infant and Preschool Child. Maltreatment of children. *The Physically Abused Child. Pediatr, 37*:377, February 1966.
8. American Humane Association: *Position Statement on Proposals for Mandatory Reporting of Suspected Inflicted Injuries on Children.* Denver, 1962.
9. American Medical Association: *Physical Abuse of Children — Suggested Legislation.* Chicago, 1965.
10. Astley, R.: Multiple metaphyseal fractures in small children. *Br J Radiol, 26*:577, 1953.
11. Bain, K.: The physically abused child. *Pediatrics, 31*:895, 1963.
12. Bakwin, H.: Multiple skeletal lesions in young children due to trauma. *J Pediatr, 49*:7, 1956.
13. Bakwin, H.: Report of the meeting of the American Humane Society. *Newsletter* (American Academy of Pediatrics), *13*:5, September-October 1962.
14. Barbero, G. J., Morris, M. G., and Redford, M. T.: Malidentification of mother-baby-father relationships expressed in infant failure to thrive. In *The Neglected-Battered Child Syndrome: Role Reversal in Parents.* New York, Child Welfare League of America, 1963.
15. Barmeyer, G. H., Anderson, L. R., and Cox, W. B.: Traumatic periostitis in young children. *J Pediatr, 38*:184, 1951.
16. Barta, R. A., and Smith, N. J.: Willful trauma to young children, a challenge to the physician. *Clin Pediatr, 2*:545, October 1963.

149

17. Battered child legislation, office of the General Counsel, A. M. A. *JAMA*, *188*:386, April 27, 1964.
18. Berlow, L.: Recognition and rescue of the battered child. *Hospitals*, *JAHA*, *41*:58, 1967.
19. Boardman, H. E.: A project to rescue children from inflicted injuries. *Social Work*, *7*:43, Jan. 1962.
20. Branigan, E., *et al.: An Exploratory Study of the Neglected Battered Child Syndrome.* Unpublished doctoral dissertation. Boston, Boston College School of Social Work, 1964.
21. Braun, I. G., *et al.:* The mistreated child. *Calif Med*, *99*:98, August 1963.
22. Bryant, H. D., *et al.:* Physical abuse of children in an agency study. *Child Welfare*, *42*:125, March 1963.
23. Caffey, J.: Multiple fractures in the long bones of infants suffering from chronic hematoma. *Am J Roentgenol Radium Ther Nucl Med*, *56*:163, August 1946.
24. Caffey, J.: Some traumatic lesions in growing bones other than fractures and dislocations: clinical and radiological features. *Br J Radiol*, *30*:225, May 1957.
25. Caffey, J.: Infantile cortical hyperostosis. *J Pediatr*, *29*:541, Nov. 1946.
26. Caffey, J.: *Journal of Pediatric X-ray Diagnosis*, 2nd ed. Chicago, Year Bk., 1950, p. 684.
27. Caffey, J.: Significance of the history in the diagnosis of traumatic injury to children. *J Pediatr*, *67*:1009, 1965.
28. Cheney, K. B.: Safeguarding legal rights in providing protective service. *Children*, *13*:86, May-June 1966.
29. Chesser, E.: *Cruelty to Children.* New York, Philosophical Library. 1952, p. 169.
30. Child abuse reporting laws. *J Am Dent Assoc*, *75*:1070, 1967.
31. Child Welfare League of America, Inc.: *The Neglected Battered Child Syndrome.* New York, July 1963.
32. Children's Bureau, U. S. Department of Health, Education, and Welfare: *The Abused Child — Principles and Suggested Language for Legislation on Reporting of the Physically Abused Child.* Washington, 1963.
33. Children's Division, The American Humane Association: *Guidelines for Legislation to Protect the Battered Child — Basic Principles and Concepts.* Denver, 1964.
34. Children's Division, The American Humane Association: *Protecting The Battered Child.* Denver, 1962.
35. Citizen's Committee for Children of New York: Child abuse (a positive statement). New York, March 1964.
36. Cohen, M. E., *et al.:* Psychological aspects of the maltreatment syndrome of childhood. *J Pediatr*, *69*:279, 1966.
37. Coleman, R. W., and Provence, S.: Environmental retardation (hospitalism) in infants living in families. *Pediatrics*, February 1957.

38. Coles, R.: Terror-stricken children. *New Republic, 150*:11, May 1964.
39. Connell, J. R.: The devil's battered children. *J Kansas Med Soc, 64*:385, Sept. 1963.
40. Curtis, G. C.: Violence breeds violence — perhaps. *Am J Psychiatr, 120*:386, October 1963.
41. De Francis, V.: *Child Abuse — Preview of a Nationwide Survey.* Children's Division, American Humane Association, Colorado, 1963.
42. De Francis, V.: Laws for mandatory reporting of child abuse cases. *State Government, 39*:8, Winter, 1966.
43. De Francis, V.: *Review of Legislation to Protect the Battered Child, a Study of Laws Enacted in 1963.* Denver, American Humane Assocation, 1964.
44. Delaney, D. W.: The physically abused child. *World Med J, 13*:145, Sept.-Oct., 1966.
45. Delsordo, J. D.: Protective casework for abused children. *Children, 10*:213, Nov.-Dec., 1963.
46. Dine, M. S.: Tranquilizer poisoning: An example of child abuse. *Pediatrics, 36*:782, 1965.
47. Duncan, G. M., Frazier, S. H., Litin, E. M., Johnson, A. M., and Barron, A. J.: Etiological factors in first-degree murder. *JAMA, 168*:1755, 1958.
48. Earl, H. G.: 10,000 children battered and starved. *Today's Health, 43*:26, 1965.
49. Easson, W. M., and Steinhilber, R. N.: Murderous aggression by children and adolescents. *Arch Gen Psychiatry, (Chicago), 4*:47, 1961.
50. Elbin, A. J., *et al.:* Battered child syndrome at Los Angeles County General Hospital. *Am J Dis Child, 118*:660, 1969.
51. Editorial. *JAMA, 176*:942, 1961.
52. Editorial. *JAMA, 181*:42, 1962.
53. Eisentein, E. M., Delta, B. G., and Clifford, J. H.: Jejunal hematoma: An unusual manifestation of the battered child syndrome. *Clin Pediatr, 4*:436, 1965.
54. Elmer, E.: Abused young children seen in hospital. *Social Work, 4*:98, October 1960.
55. Elmer, E., *et al.:* Developmental characteristics of abused children. *Pediatrics, 40*:596, 1967.
56. Elmer, E.: Hazards in determining child abuse. *Child Welfare,* Jan. 1966, p. 28.
57. Elmer, E.: Identification of abused children. *Children,* September-October 1963, p. 180.
58. Elmer, E.: *Children in Jeopardy.* Pittsburgh, Univ of Pittsburgh, 1967.
59. Fairburn, A. C., and Hunt, A. C.: Caffey's third syndrome — a critical evaluation ("the battered baby"). *Med Sci Law, 4*:123, April 1964.
60. Family Court of the State of New York, City of New York: Statistical report for the month of December, 1963, p. 2.
61. Finberg, L.: A pediatrician's view of the abused child. *Child Welfare,*

Jan. 1965, p. 41.
62. Fisher, S. H.: Skeletal manifestations of parent-induced trauma in infants and children. *Southern Med J, 51*:956, 1958.
63. Flato, C.: Parents who beat children. *Saturday Evening Post, 235*:30, 1962.
64. Fontana, V. J.: The "maltreatment syndrome" in children. *N Engl J Med, 269*:1389, 1963.
65. Fontana, V. J.: *The Maltreated Child,* 1st ed. Springfield, Thomas, 1964.
66. Fontana, V. J.: The neglect and abuse of children. *N Y State J Med, 64*:215, 1964.
67. Fontana, V. J.: An insidious and disturbing medical entity. *Public Welfare,* July 1966, p. 235.
68. Fontana, V. J.: Further reflections on maltreatment of children. *N Y State J Med, 68*:2214, 1968.
69. Foster, H. H., and Freed, D. J.: Battered child legislation and professional immunity. *Am Bar Assoc J, 52*:1071, 1966.
70. Fowler, F. V.: The physician, the battered child and the law. *Pediatrics, 31*:488, August 1963.
71. Frauenberger, G. S., and Lis, E. F.: Multiple fractures associated with subdural hematoma in infancy. *Pediatrics, 6*:890, 1950.
72. Friedman, M.: Traumatic periostitis in infants and children. *JAMA, 166*:1840, 1958.
73. Fulk, D. L.: The battered child. *Nurs Forum, 3*:10, 1964.
74. Gil, D. C.: *Epidemiologic Study of Child Abuse* — research in progress. Brandeis University, 1965.
75. Gil, D. G.: What schools can do about child abuse. *Outlook,* February 1970.
76. Gluckman, L. K.: Cruelty to children. *N Z Med J, 67*:153, 1968.
77. Green, A. H.: Self-destructive behavior in physically abused schizophrenia children. Report of cases. *Arch Gen Psychiatry (Chicago), 19*:171, 1968.
78. Greengord, J.: The battered child syndrome. *Med Sci, 15*:82, 1964.
79. Greengord, J.: Child abuse: second look after state legislation. *Med Sci, 18*:32, 1967.
80. Gregg, G. S., and Elmer, E.: Infant injuries: accident or abuse? *Pediat, 44*:434, 1969.
81. Gwinn, J. L., Lewin, K. W., and Peterson, H. G., Jr.: Roentgenographic manifestations of unsuspected trauma in infancy. *JAMA, 176*:926, 1961.
82. Hall, G. B.: Battered child reporting laws — medicolegal considerations. *The Doctor and the Law,* a monthly medicolegal newsletter. Wyeth Laboratories, June 1966.
83. Hamlin, H.: Subgaleal hematoma caused by hair-pull. *JAMA, 204*:339, 1968.
84. Hanson, R. H.: Child abuse legislation and the interdisciplinary approach. *Am Bar Assoc J, 52*:734, 1966.

85. Helfer, R., and Kempe, C. H. (Eds.): *The Battered Child.* Chicago, U. of Chicago, 1968.

86. Helfer, R., *et al.:* The battered child syndrome. *Adv Pediatr, 15:*9, 1968.

87. Helfer, R.: Physicians told how to deal with child abuse. *JAMA, 211:*35, 1970.

88. Hoel, H. W.: The battered child. *Minn Med, 46:*1001, 1963.

89. Holter, J. C., *et al.:* Child abuse: early case findings in the emergency department. *Pediatrics, 42:*128, 1968.

90. Holter, J. C. and Freidman, S. B.: Principles of management in child abuse cases. *Am J Orthopsychiatry, 38:*127, 1968.

91. Isaacs, S.: Physical ill-treatment of children. *Lancet, 1:*37, 1968.

92. Jacobziner, J.: Rescuing the battered child. *Am J Nurs, 64:*92, 1964.

93. Johnson, B., *et al.:* Injured children and their parents. *Children, 15:*147, 1968.

94. Jones, H. H., and Davis, J. H.: Multiple traumatic lesions of the infant skeleton. *Stanford Med Bull, 15:*259, 1957.

95. Kaplan, M.: Deaths of young studied by city. *New York Times,* May 5, 1962.

96. Kempe, C. H., Silverman, F. N., Steele, B. F., Droegemueller, W., and Silver, H. K.: The battered child syndrome. *JAMA, 181:*17, 1962.

97. Kempe, C. H.: The battered child and the hospital. *Hosp Practice,* October 1969, p. 44.

98. Kim, T.: Pseudocyst of the pancreas as a manifestation of the battered child syndrome. *Med Ann DC, 36:*664, 1967.

99. Koel, B. S.: Failure to thrive and fatal injury as a continuum. *Am J Dis Child, 118:*563, 1969.

100. Krywulnk, W., *et al.:* The physically abused child. *Manitoba Med Rev, 47:*472, 1967.

101. Kunstadter, R. H., *et al.:* The battered child and the celiac syndrome. *Ill Med J, 132:*267, 1967.

102. Lesermann, S.: There's a murderer in my waiting room. *Med Econ, 41:*62, 1964.

103. Lewis, H.: Parental and community neglect: twin responsibilities of protective services. *Children, 16:*114, 1969.

104. Maltreatment of children: The physically abused child. Committee on Infant and Pre-school Child. American Academy of Pediatrics. *Pediatrics, 37:*377, 1966.

105. Marie, J., *et al.:* Hematome sousdural due nourrisson accocie a des fractures des membres. *Sem Hop Paris, 30:*1757, 1954.

106. Marquezy, R. A., Bach, C., and Blondeau, M.: Himatome sousdural et fractures multiples des os longs chez un nowvission de N. mois. *Arch Fr Pediatr, 9:*526, 1952.

107. McHenry, T., Girdany, B. R., and Elmer, E.: Unsuspected trauma with multiple skeletal injuries during infancy and childhood. *Pediatrics, 31:*903, 1963.

108. McKown, C. H., Verhulst, H. L., and Crotty, J. J.: Overdosage effects and danger from tranquilizing drugs. *JAMA, 185*:425, 1963.
109. Merrill, E. J.: *Physical Abuse of Children: An Agency Study in Protecting the Battered Child.* Denver, Children's Division, American Humane Association, 1962.
110. Miller, D. S.: Fractures among children. *Minn Med, 42*:1209, 1959.
111. Milowe, I. D.: *Patterns of Parental Behavior Leading to Physical Abuse of Children.* Presented at Workshop sponsored by the Children's Bureau in collaboration with the University of Colorado, Colorado Springs, March 21, 22, 1966.
112. Milowe, I. D., and Louri, R. S.: The child's role in the battered child syndrome. *J Pediatr, 65*:1079, 1964.
113. Morris, M. G., and Gould, R. W.: Role reversal: A necessary concept in dealing with the "battered child syndrome". *Am J Orthopsychiatry, 33*:298, 1963.
114. Morris, M. G., Gould, R. W., and Matthews, P. J.: Toward prevention of child abuse. *Children, 11*:55, 1964.
115. News Report. *Med World News,* 2:30, October 27, 1961.
116. *New York Medicine.* M. D. responsibility for the protection of the battered child. *26*:59, 1970.
117. *New York Medicine.* Rise in babies with narcotics addiction. July 1966, p. 1767.
118. Odlum, D. M.: Neglected children. *R Soc Health J, 79*:737, 1959.
119. Oettinger, K. B.: Protecting children from abuse. *Parents Magazine, 39*:12, 1964.
120. Ott, J. F.: Neglected or physically abused children, a review. *J S Carolina Med Ass, 60*:309, 1964.
121. Patton, R. G., and Gardner, L. I.: *Growth Failure in Maternal Deprivation.* Springfield, Thomas, 1963.
122. Paull, D., et al.: A new approach to reporting child abuse. *Hospitals, 41*:62, 1967.
123. Paulsen, M. G., et al.: Child abuse reporting laws — some legislative history. *George Washington Law Rev, 34*:482, 1966.
124. Paulsen, M. G.: Legal framework of child protection. *Columbia Law Rev,* April 1966.
125. Paulsen, M. G.: Legal protections against child abuse. *Children, 13*:42, 1966.
126. *Pediatric Currents* (Ross Laboratories). Failure to thrive. *18*:57, September 1969.
127. Pfundt, T. R.: The problem of the battered child. *Postgrad Med, 35*:426, 1964.
128. Pickle, S., Anderson, C. C., and Holliday, M. A.: Thirsting and hypernatremic dehydration — a form of child abuse. *Pediatrics, 45*:54, 1970.
129. *Planning for the Protection and Care of Neglected Children in*

California. Sacramento, National Study Service, 1964.

130. *Preventive and Protective Services to Children, a Responsibility of the Public Welfare Agency*. Chicago, Amer. Public Welfare Association, 1958.

131. Reinitz, F. G.: Special registration project on the abused child. *Child Welfare, 44*:103, 1965.

132. Reiner, B. S., and Kaufman, I.: *Character Disorders in Parents of Delinquents*. New York, Family Service Association of America, 1959.

133. Reinhart, J. B., and Elmer, R.: The abused child: mandatory reporting legislation, *JAMA, 188*:358, 1964.

134. Russell, D. H.: Law, medicine and minors. *N Engl J Med, 279*:31, 1968.

135. Schachter, M.: Contribution to the clinical and psychological study of mistreated children: physical and moral cruelty. *G Psichiat Neuropat, 80*:311, 1952.

136. Schleyer, F., and Pioch, W.: Fatal outcome by crush syndrome after continuous beatings of a child. *Monatsschr Kinderheilkd, 105*:393, 1957.

137. Schloesser, P. T.: The abused child. *Bull Menninger Clin, 28*:260, 1964.

138. Schrotel, S. R.: Responsibilities of physicians in suspected cases of brutality. *Cinn J Med, 42*:406, 1961.

139. Sheriff, H.: The abused child. *J Carolina Med Ass, 60*:191, 1964.

140. Shaw, A.: How to help the battered child. *RISS, 6*:71, 1963.

141. Silver, H. K., and Kempe, C. H.: The problem of parental criminal neglect and severe physical abuse of children. *Am J Dis Child, 98*:528, 1959.

142. Silver, L. B.: Child abuse syndrome: a review. *Med Times, 196*:803, 1968.

143. Silver, L. B., Barton, W., and Dublin, C. C.: Child abuse laws — are they enough? *JAMA, 199*:65, 1967.

144. Silver, L. B., Dublin, C. C., and Lourie, R. S.: Does violence breed violence? Contributions from a study of the child abuse syndrome. *Am J Psychiatry, 126*:404, 1969.

145. Silverman, F. N.: The roentgen manifestations of unrecognized skeletal trauma in infants. *Am J Roentgenol Radium Ther Nucl Med, 69*:413, 1953.

146. Simons, B., and Downs, E. F.: Medical reporting of child abuse patterns, problems and accomplishments. *N Y J Med, 68*:2324, 1968.

147. Simpson, K. S.: The battered baby problem. *Afr J Med Sci, 42*:661, 1968.

148. Smith, A. E.: The beaten child. *Hygeia, 22*:386, 1944.

149. Smith, M. J.: Subdural hematoma with multiple fractures. *Am J Roentgenol Radium Ther Nucl Med, 63*:342, 1950.

150. Snedecor, S. T., Knapp, R. E., and Wilson, H. B.: Traumatic ossifying periostitis of newborn. *Surg Gynecol Obstet, 61*:385, 1935.

151. Snedecor, S. T., and Wilson, H. B.: Some obstetrical injuries to long bones. *J Bone Joint Surg* [Amer], *31A*:378, 1949.

152. Snedeker, L.: Traumatization of children. *N Engl J Med, 267*:572, 1962.

153. Stone, J. S.: Acute epiphyseal and periosteal infections in infants and children. *Boston Med Surg J, 156*:842, 1907.

154. Sullivan E., *et al.:* Symposium: Battered child syndrome. *Clin Pro Child Hosp DC, 20*:229, 1964.

155. Sussman, S. J.: Skin manifestations of the battered child syndrome. *J Pediatr, 72*:99, 1968.

156. Sussman, S. J.: The battered child syndrome. *Calif Med, 108*:437, 1968.

157. Swischuk, L. E.: Spine and spinal cord trauma in the battered child syndrome. *Radiology, 92*:733, 1969.

158. Ten Bensel, R. W., and Raile, R. B.: The battered child syndrome. *Minn Med, 46*:977, 1963.

159. Terr, L. C., *et al.:* The battered child rebrutalized: ten cases of medical-legal confusion. *Am J Psychiatry, 124*:1432, 1968.

160. Till, K.: Subdural haematoma on effusion in infancy. *Br Med J, 3*:804, 1968.

161. Toland, M.: Abuse of children — whose responsibility. *Conn Med, 28*:438, 1964.

162. Touloukian, R. J.: Visceral injury caused by trauma. *Mod Med,* November 1969.

163. U. S. Children's Bureau. Clearinghouse for Research in Child Life: *Bibliography on the Battered Child.* Washington. (Revised periodically).

164. U. S. Department of Health, Education and Welfare. Welfare Administration, Children's Bureau. *The Abused Child: Principles and Suggested Language for Legislation on Reporting of the Physically Abused Child,* Washington, 1963.

165. Wadlington, Walter: A new look at the courts and children's rights. *Children, 16*:138, 1969.

166. Wasserman, S.: The abused parent and abused child. *Children, 14*:175, 1967.

167. West, S.: Acute periosteal swelling in several young infants of the same family, probably rickety in nature. *Br Med J, 1*:856, 1888.

168. Weston, W. J.: Metaphyseal fractures in infancy. *J Bone and Joint Surg* [Brit], *39B*:694, 1957.

169. *What's New* (Abbott Laboratories). Willful injuries to children. No. 228, Summer 1962.

170. Wilson, R. A.: Legal action and the "battered child". (Letter to the Editor). *Pediatrics, 33*:1003, 1964.

171. Woolley, P. V., Jr.: The pediatrician and the young child subjected to repeated physical abuse. *J Pediatr, 62*:628, 1963.

172. Woolley, P. V., Jr., and Evans, W. A., Jr.: Significance of skeletal lesions in infants resembling those of traumatic origin. *JAMA, 158*:539, 1955.

173. Young, L.: *Wednesday's Children: A Study of Child Abuse and Neglect.* New York, McGraw, 1964.

174. Zalba, S. R.: The abused child: 1. A survey of the problem. *Social Work, 11*:3, 1966.

Selected Resources

Books

Arnold, L. Eugene (Ed.): Helping parents help their children. New York, Brunner/Mazel, 1978.

Besharov, Douglas J.: Juvenile justice advocacy. New York, Practising Law Institute, 1974.

Fontana, Vincent J.: Somewhere a child is crying. New York, Macmillan, (hardcover), 1973; New York, Mentor (paperback), 1976.

Kempe, C. H., and Kempe, R. S.: Child abuse. Cambridge, Massachusetts, Harvard University Press, 1978.

Kempe, C. Henry, and Helfer, Ray E. (Eds.): Helping the battered child and his family. Philadelphia, Lippincott, 1972.

Kempe, C. Henry, and Helfer, Ray E. (Eds.): Child abuse and neglect: The family and the community. Cambridge, Ballinger, 1976.

Nagi, S. Z.: Child maltreatment in United States: A challenge to social institutions. New York, Columbia University Press, 1977.

National Committee for Prevention of Child Abuse: National directory of child abuse services and information. Chicago, 1974.

Susman, A., and Cohen, S. J.: Reporting child abuse and neglect. Cambridge, Ballinger, 1975.

U. S. National Center on Child Abuse and Neglect (HEW): Child abuse and neglect programs. U. S. Govt. Print Office, Washington, 1976.

Information Centers

The American Humane Association, Children's Division (AHA), 5351 S. Roslyn Street, Englewood, Colorado 80110.

Child Abuse Treatment and Prevention Program, New York Foundling Hospital Center for Parent and Child Development, 1175 Third Avenue, New York, New York 10021.

Center for the Prevention and Treatment of Child Abuse and Neglect, Department of Pediatrics, University of Colorado Medical Center, 1205 Oneida Street, Denver, Colorado 80220.

National Committee for Prevention of Child Abuse, Box 2866, Chicago, Illinois 60690.

United States National Center of Child Abuse and Neglect (NCCAN), Office of Child Development (HEW), P.O. Box 1182, Washington, D.C. 20013.

NAME INDEX

SUBJECT INDEX

A

Abandonment, 3, 85, 102, 148
Abdominal trauma, 17
Abrasions, 16, 131-133, 143
Abscess, 132
Abuse, 7 (*See also* specific types)
Abused child defined, 7
Abused victims' age, 28
Abusive parent's characteristics, 29, 32
Accidental deaths, 10
Accidental trauma, 22-23
Adolescents (*See also* Teenagers)
  abuse of, 28-29
  pregnant population of, 57-58
  sexual exploitation, 29
After Care, 64
Agency operated boarding home, 65
Aggressive parent, 29
Alcoholism, 25, 29
American Academy of Pediatrics, 4
Committee on Infant and Pre-School Child, 5, 70
American Humane Society, 4, 28
Children's Division, 11, 25, 40-42
  Advisory Committee to, recommendations of, 69
American Society for the Prevention of Cruelty to Animals, 14
Anemia, 16, 132-133, 142, 148
Animalistic instincts, 3
Arts and crafts course, 63
At risk potential of families, 58

B

Battered child
  defined, 15-16
  number of, 11
  plight of, 79
Battered child syndrome, 4, 15

Battering parent as battered child of yesterday, 27, 29
Beatings, 33, 133, 143
Birth control, 3
Bite marks, human, 18
Black eyes, 20
Blindness, 132
Blue sclera, 23
Bonding, 56
Bone changes, 20-21
Bone injury, evidence of, 19
Bone repair, evidence of, 19
Bowel, rupture of, 17
Brain damage, 10
Brain disease (*See* Organic brain disease)
Brain injuries, 11
Bronx County Society for the Prevention of Cruelty to Children in New York, 11
Bruises (*See* Ecchymosis)
Burn wounds, 33-34
Burns, 16, 33, 133-134, 147

C

Calcification, 20, 136, 138
CALM hotline functions, 50
Cancer, 10
Case reports, 130-148
Central nervous system irritation, 18
Central register of child protection cases, 73, 79, 97-98, 120, 124
  confidentiality, 98, 122-123, 125-127
  right to privacy, 98, 123-124
Cephalohematoma, 144
Cerebral edema, 131
Character personality of abusing parent, 26
Child abuse (*See also* Maltreatment syndrome in children)
  courses taught in, 51

163